Dr. Pollard

Opera Guide 34

Linda Esther Gray as Kundry and Warren Ellsworth as Parsifal at Welsh National Opera; producer, Mike Ashman; designer, Peter Mumford (photo: Clive Barda)

Preface

This series, published under the auspices of English National Opera and The Royal Opera, aims to prepare audiences to evaluate and enjoy opera performances. Each book contains the complete text, set out in the original language together with a current performing translation. The accompanying essays have been commissioned as general introductions to aspects of interest in each work. As many illustrations and musical examples as possible have been included because the sound and spectacle of opera are clearly central to any sympathetic appreciation of it. We hope that, as companions to the opera should be, they are well-informed, witty and attractive.

Nicholas John
Series Editor

34

Parsifal

Richard Wagner

Opera Guide Series Editor: Nicholas John

Published in association with
English National Opera and The Royal Opera

John Calder · London
Riverrun Press · New York

First published in Great Britain, 1986 by
John Calder (Publishers) Ltd.,
18 Brewer Street, London W1R 4AS

First published in the U.S.A., 1986 by
Riverrun Press Inc.,
1170 Broadway,
New York, NY 10001

BRITISH LIBRARY CATALOGUING IN PUBLICATION DATA

Wagner, Richard, *1813—1883*.
 Parsifal.—(English National Opera guides; 34)
 1. Wagner, Richard, *1813—1883*. Parsifal
 2. Operas—Librettos
 I. Title   II. Porter, Andrew   III. English National Opera
 IV.Royal Opera   V. Series
 782.1′092′4   ML410.W17

ISBN 0-7145-4079-X

Typeset in Plantin by Margaret Spooner Typesetting, Bridport, Dorset.

Printed by Camelot Press Ltd., Southampton.

Contents

List of Illustrations

A Very Human Epic

Mike Ashman

Parsifal has been variously praised — or dismissed — as a Christian work, a National Socialist work, a tired valedictory or, in Ernest Newman's words, 'the supreme song of love and pity'.

Toscanini is reported to have said in later life that he would not give performances of *The Barber of Seville* because audiences and critics would not accept what they would hear under his baton: the distortions of traditional performances had reached a point where people would no longer recognise the pure score of the work itself. A similar gap of expectation exists in the case of *Parsifal*, although it is not by and large a musical one. It was Nietzsche, that perfect anti-Wagnerite, who initiated the series of attacks and commentaries on the text of Wagner's last drama that have laid a thick ideological and interpretative mist over readings of the piece. In addition, despite the fact that *Parsifal* represents the most sophisticated essay by a composer whose creative life was dedicated to the resolution of the fascinating relationship between words and music in drama, a huge critical gulf has widened between commentaries on the work's music and on its text — a gulf typified by Debussy who enjoyed himself in print[1] poking fun at what he saw as the text's sacramental pretensions but made almost embarrassing obeisance to the actual score, calling it 'one of the most beautiful edifices in sound ever raised to the glory of music'.

The first confusion may well stem from Wagner himself. He titled the work *Bühnenweihfestspiel* — which means not so much 'sacred festival drama' (a standard English rendering) but rather 'festival work to consecrate a stage'. The 'stage' was, of course, Bayreuth and the 'consecration' was for Wagner's heirs. He did not mean to enshrine *Parsifal* as the High Mass of some exclusivist (or ideologically sinister) cult at the temple of Bayreuth but he did want Cosima and Siegfried to have something to make money from (and repay the debts which threatened the life of the festival) in an age when royalties and copyright were far from secure. His typically intense letters to King Ludwig about 'scorning the Grail's solace' and the fear of making public a work 'in which the most profound mysteries of the Christian faith are enacted on the stage' may be seen as propaganda exercises in mysticism, aimed at financial security for the Wagner family. There were purely artistic reasons, of course, for maintaining Bayreuth's monopoly of the work: Wagner's mature works were not well represented in the German theatres of the 1880s either by adequate stagings or by frequency of performance. Even Angelo Neumann's officially approved touring *Ring* production played *Rhinegold* with an interval. Basically, however, the composer's attempt to put wraps around his new score was for reasons of financial self-preservation.

Pace generations of (mostly British) critical opinion, *Parsifal* is *not* a 'religious' or 'Christian' work, any more than *The Ring* is a 'Nordic' or 'Scandinavian' work, or *Tristan* a 'Breton' or 'Celtic' work. Nietzsche, preparing himself for the atheistic debate of his *Also Sprach Zarathustra*, is said to have complained of a moral and artistic 'sell-out' in *Parsifal*: 'Wagner

---

1. In his collected music criticism, reprinted in English as *Monsieur Croche, the Dilettante Hater* (Dover, 1962). Some of his reviews were actually written by Colette.

has prostrated himself before the Christian cross.' He was surely confusing source and inspiration with the finished article. The sources for the *Parsifal* story are medieval poems — principally, almost uniquely, Wolfram von Eschenbach's *Parzival*,[2] a text first read by Wagner in that extraordinary period in the late 1840s when, as Pierre Boulez has noted, he effectively discovered material for his entire life's dramatic output. Wolfram's poem was set down at that interesting stage in Celtic literary history when the influence of church and state was just starting to affect the retelling of the rich body of folk material which came to Europe from Ireland via Wales and Cornwall. In the same way that Wagner carefully steered his version of the Siegfried story away from over-refining (and simplistic) Christian influences (for instance, in the *Nibelungenlied* Siegfried is characterised as a medieval knight and his death is celebrated by a High Mass in Worms Cathedral) towards an older, more truly 'epic' note, he took pains not to make the spiritual aspects in his *Parsifal* too specific.

The name 'Christ' is never mentioned in Wagner's text. We hear of 'Him' and the 'Saviour' and even 'He on the Cross'; but many other world religions, including Buddhism, embrace self-sacrificing messiahs. It is worth mentioning that the central figure of *The Ring* (and of Scandinavian mythology), Wotan/Odin, also hung on a tree for three days to gain wisdom with which to rule the world better and that a spear (carved from that tree) plays a major symbolic part in the story. Wagner was researching Buddhism when *Parsifal* was conceived, and even planning a drama with a Buddhist theme, *Die Sieger*, 'The Victors'. (He came to realise that the subject matter of this drama — the Schopenhauerian idea of renunciation of selfish interest as the highest goal in life — had been exhausted by his work on *Parsifal*.) Moreover, the symbols of a 'grail', a spear which delivers a wound in the side and a magical Love Feast are far from being uniquely Christian. They have clear antecedents in Celtic folk stories. Wagner may have made the stage property of his 'grail' look like a chalice but it has most of the pagan properties of the 'horn of plenty' of the Welsh King Bran the Blessed or the cowl of Anwen, from which the Holy Grail mythologically derives. This horn, cowl or grail ('grail' really meaning just any serving vessel) had the power of giving eternal sustenance to those who fed or drank from it. In his mind Wagner clearly equated his spear with that of the Roman soldier Longinus who pierced the side of Christ on the cross — although this is nowhere stated categorically in the text. In the majority of the Grail legend sources, including Wolfram, the redeemer hero has to ask the right questions about the Grail king's suffering before he can 'heal' him. When he fails to do so on his first visit to the castle, he is summarily ejected and faces years of wandering before realising his missed opportunity (i.e. that he had actually seen the Grail). He returns, asks the questions and assumes leadership of the Grail order. The tale is a basic metaphor for the acquiring of wisdom, maturity and compassion in life. Wagner was worried about the dramatic force of these 'questions' and kept this idea only by implication — Gurnemanz's frustration that Parsifal has seen all the events of the Love Feast and yet said or done nothing. To motivate Parsifal's quest more clearly, he took over the idea of the overthrow of a magic castle from another limb of the Grail stories (the hero of this section in Wolfram is actually Gawan) and joined the two elements together by the device of recovering the lost Spear. (In

2. Wagner certainly read a contemporary commentary on the *Parzival* text by San-Marte but it remains unclear how well he knew the (earlier) French sources by Chrétien de Troyes and its 'completions' by Robert de Boron and others.

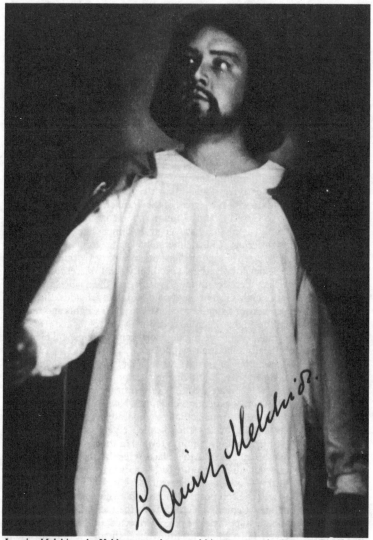

Lauritz Melchior, the Heldentenor who started his career as a baritone, as Parsifal. He sang Tristan over 200 times. (Royal Opera House Archives)

Wolfram the Spear is never lost to the Grail brethren.) And the 'wound' which Amfortas receives when Klingsor takes the Spear from him has rather less to do with Christ's wound than with the Celtic myths of an infertile (Grail) king, and hence an infertile kingdom awaiting a saviour. In other words, Amfortas is wounded in the genitals, not in the side — a fact hinted at in Wagner's first prose draft of the drama and seemingly confirmed by rehearsal accounts of the Wagner family (such as that of Daniela von Bülow when directing Herbert Janssen in the 1930s). It is hard to say whether prudish conventions or a deliberate desire for ambiguity stopped Wagner establishing this fact. Either way, there is a profitable gain in suggestive imagery and the parallel between

Klingsor and Amfortas (the 'black' and the 'white', or the Alberich and the Wotan, of *Parsifal*) becomes even clearer: both have been effectively 'unmanned' by sexual lust. It would be an interesting dramaturgical experiment to double the role in performance, rather like Venus and Elisabeth in *Tannhäuser*.

Other elements in Wagner's text show how Christian imagery is used but not merely imitated. The composer did indeed visit a Catholic priest in Munich to check on details of the liturgy and the Mass but no words of ritual in his Act One Grail scene are taken directly from that (or indeed any other) liturgy. The 'great Communion scene' which British writers at the turn of the century were so fond of praising — even fasting and praying before attending performances! — is a figment of their imaginations. The 'baptism' of Parsifal and Kundry, and the annointing of Parsifal in Act Three, use the elements of oil and water present in initiation ceremonies since recorded time. The story which Kundry confesses in Act Two — 'I saw Him . . . Him . . . and laughed' — is an ingenious mixture of the legend of the Wandering Jew (who mocked Christ on the way to Calvary) and the many moments in Eastern folklore when characters only come to discover true compassion after showing contempt for the suffering. The deliberately vague geographical setting 'landscape *in the character of* the northern mountains of Gothic Spain' (my italics) — recalls medieval holy wars, specifically the 13th-century crusade against the Albigensian 'heretics' in the Pyrenees, but the challenge Klingsor presents to the Grail knights is more psychological than religious. Finally, an example from the composer's stage directions: the Grail knights and servants should look 'similar to Knights Templars . . . but, instead of the red cross, they should have the symbol of a hovering dove on their weapons and cloaks'. A dove is not a specifically Christian symbol.

The debate as to whether or not the text of *Parsifal* embodies a gospel of anti-semitic racial superiority — anticipating the practices of Hitler's Third Reich — has recently threatened to gain a stranglehold on German 'musicological' writing on Wagner (see end note). No sane commentator can now doubt that Wagner was, intellectually at any rate, a bigoted anti-semite or that the writings of his last years (the so-called 'regeneration' essays of the *Religion and Art* sequence) show leanings towards a theory of a superior and pure Aryan race. No defence against these facts is tenable. Nevertheless, what some writers — especially the inaccurate Robert Gutman[3] and the Nietzsche-like Hartmut Zelinsky — overlook is the extent (or lack of it) to which these prose works influenced the composition of *Parsifal*, whose text was complete in all essentials before Wagner's meetings with the racist Count Arthur de Gobineau[4] (whose basic hypothesis he politely rejected) or the setting down of the essays themselves. Throughout his life Wagner the music dramatist kept some creative distance from Wagner the prentice politician and philosopher. It is not within the scope of this article to debate Gutman's and Zelinsky's farcical belief that Wagner's entire artistic credo *was* anti-semitism — they would do better to aim their critical guns at the likes of Houston Stewart Chamberlain and other Bayreuth 'disciples' — but it is relevant to point out

3. Gutman muddles the chronology of the various essays written by Wagner in the *Religion and Art* group and incorrectly dates Wagner's meetings with Gobineau.

4. Gobineau's (1816-82) magnum opus, *Essai sur l'inégalité des races humaines* (1853-55) was given a new lease of life by Wagner's interest; its main thesis was the supposed degeneration of (European) man through breeding with inferior races.

Marianne Brandt (above), one of the three singers to take the role of Kundry at Bayreuth in 1882, and (below) Kirsten Flagstad as Kundry (photos: Royal Opera House Archives and Angus McBean © Harvard Theatre Collection)

that all the 'fascist' elements in *Parsifal* are specifically criticised, attacked and defeated within the action of the drama.

And what are these 'fascist' elements? (Let us use this term for easy reference even if it is historically anachronistic.) In keeping with his mythological sources' idea of a land (and a people) made barren by the infertility of the king, Wagner shows the Grail brethren in a most hostile light: a decaying society turned in on itself. As Wieland Wagner pointed out at the time of his famous 1950s Bayreuth production, this society is already in danger before the curtain rises: Titurel has misused his guardianship of the 'holy' relics (grail, spear) for 'mental satisfaction and prolongation of life'. He has also found no relationship with the *third* 'gift' God sent him — Kundry, a woman — treating her as merely a servant-messenger.[5] Not until Parsifal returns to the Grail castle at the climax of Act Three with the spear *and* Kundry can what was misunderstood and lost be made whole. When Amfortas, like an over-brash Henry V suffering defeat at Agincourt, loses the spear to Klingsor, the Grail realm lapses further into a state of vicious brooding — note the squires' aggression towards Kundry, their meaningless 'Boys' Own' heroic statements about recovering the spear during Gurnemanz's narration, the knights' state-police attitude towards Parsifal's intrusion (and their sentimentality about the swan). Even Gurnemanz, once Titurel's squire and evidently then a fighting man, is tainted by worry that Amfortas is no longer 'siegreich' (literally, 'rich in victorious conquest'), and clings onto the first straw of hope that appears. He then fails to see, by the end of Act One, that Parsifal has all the qualities of a 'pure fool'. Yet this is hardly surprising in a society where all initiative is punished — Klingsor for trying too hard to be 'pure', or the unseen Gawan for leaving (unbidden) to seek a remedy for Amfortas's wound.

By the time we hear the bells of Monsalvat for the second time, the brethren have abandoned any pretence at crusading for the good of man. Titurel has died; missions have been abandoned. Wagner significantly directs that the eating tables for the Love Feast be absent from this scene and that the knights appear armed in the Grail hall. Could this be a right-wing coup, prepared to force the sickly Amfortas to do his duty (i.e. to unveil the grail, the quick 'hit' that keeps the brothers alive) and to face the consequences if he refuses? Then Parsifal returns, not, however, to restore the old order but to initiate a new one: 'It [the grail] shall never more be shut away. Unveil the grail. *Open the shrine!*' (my translation and italics). All this seems to point towards the very antithesis of any National Socialist creed.

Other moments in the text have been questioned on ideological grounds. Amfortas's 'blood' imagery in 'Wehvolles Erbe' — he contrasts his own 'sinful' blood with the 'divine fount' of pure blood present at the unveiling of the grail — is surely no more than a metaphor of remorse for the manner in which he gained his wound. The almost racial taunts thrown by the Grail squires at Kundry and Klingsor are shown for the worthless cant they are. Parsifal's rejection of Kundry in Act Two is not intended to be a condemnation of all sexual activity (or of contact with the opposite sex) but a healer's method of freeing her from the psychological trap into which she has fallen (i.e. self-salvation through seduction). Kundry's 'Dienen, dienen'

5. Gurnemanz tells the squires that Titurel found Kundry on the spot where he was building the castle. She was 'asleep in the undergrowth in the wood, numb, lifeless, as if dead . . .'. I am indeed indebted to the singer Linda Esther Gray for pointing out that she thus came to Titurel at the same time and in the same place as the holy relics of the grail and the spear.

('Serving, serving') in Act Three is not an anti-feminist sentence for life, but a depiction of the (very Buddhist) state of mind that she has now reached: she is *free* to serve in the Grail domain (if she now wishes to) and is not just doing so as a form of Jekyll and Hyde repentance for her role as Klingsor's accomplice in the battle against the 'unnaturally chaste' knights (Wieland Wagner). And Gurnemanz's 'coronation' of Parsifal is not some sinister dictatorial renewal of power within a closed society but a continuation of his role as baptiser. He is Hans Sachs to Parsifal's Walther von Stolzing, inaugurating the birth of a 'mastersong' of a new era for the Grail brethren and the world they will serve once more.

The idea that *Parsifal* is some kind of tired farewell to life, showing only intermittent traces of Wagner's former fire and genius, is based on the same kind of misunderstanding that surrounds Shakespeare's last plays (such as *The Winter's Tale* or *The Tempest*) and sees them as inferior to the tragic 'masterpieces' like *Lear* and *Hamlet*. The parallel is a very close one, as befits an example using a dramatist very dear to Wagner's heart. Simply stated, dramas like *The Ring* and *Lear* portray events building towards a catharsis which is normally followed by a resolution implying some hope for the future. The 'drama' itself is created by 'tragic' actions — *e.g.* the deaths of Siegmund or Cordelia, Lear's abdication or the theft of the gold — which occupy the majority of the playing time; the resolution is normally comparatively brief, *viz.* Fortinbras's speech, Brünnhilde's immolation. In *Parsifal* and *The Tempest* Wagner and Shakespeare begin with a world in which the major tragic events have already taken place before the curtain rises: the Spear has been lost, Prospero has been deposed. The resolution of this catharsis thus becomes the main part of the dramatic action — and leads eventually to a more complete (second) 'resolution' than was possible at the end of the 'tragic' works. Dramatic tension is here used in a different manner. A great deal of material has to be presented to an audience in the form of retrospective narration (a device which Wagner's Greek-influenced dramaturgy was supremely well-equipped to use), and the (happy) end of the story is to an extent predicted and known in advance. This difference has fooled even supposed admirers of *Parsifal* into stating that nothing 'happens' until the hero's arrow strikes the swan a little less than half-way through Act One. In fact the piecemeal manner in which Gurnemanz, prompted by the squires and the appearance of Kundry, narrates the circumstances in which the Spear was lost — and almost manages to work out Kundry's role in these events — has all the tension of a 'modern' psychological thriller: a kind of 'who *will* do it?'.

The astonishingly advanced nature of Wagner's dramaturgy has received far too little critical attention. His narrative methods and dramatic dialogues parallel Ibsen and Flaubert and anticipate Proust. Form is of far greater importance than content: it is not 'what' happens but how people relate to that 'what' that is of interest. The back-narrations in *The Ring* are not a careless editing hangover from the time when the work was planned as first one, then two, then four dramas: they are the nodal points for building character and tension, replacing the 'aside' aria monologues of the then contemporary grand opera. And in *Parsifal* Act One, as indicated above, the back-narration is deliberately fragmented and distorted to create tension. Furthermore, although *Parsifal* is an epic tale, empty 'heroic' action is banished totally and even disparaged. Siegfried's 'neuen Taten' ('new deeds') have become Parsifal's 'wilden Knabentaten' ('wild boyish deeds').

In the same way that Shakespeare's last plays may be seen as alternative solutions to themes proposed in earlier works — compare the jealousy of Othello with that of Leontes in *The Winter's Tale*, or the forced abdications of the kings in *Lear* and *The Tempest* — so may *Parsifal* be seen as another version of *Götterdämmerung*, especially of the 'optimistic' ending that Wagner planned in 1848. The Grail brotherhood is an earthly Valhalla for 'chosen' heroes and the drama that follows an examination of the problems that such a fantastic Utopia would pose. By the 1880s Wagner had almost returned to the more humanistic, more 'socialist' ideas of his angry younger days in Dresden and that is why Newman's 'supreme song of love and pity' is both too simple and too mystifying a comment on Parsifal.

The stage panoply of the Grail scenes or the ballet of Klingsor's Flower Maidens should not make us forget the human element in the drama. Gurnemanz is not a perfect, saintly hermit — like Wolfram von Eschenbach's Trevrizent — but an earthy, frustrated man of action who, even in his Good Friday 'lecture' to Parsifal about sorrowing nature, uses the imagery of a layman. Amfortas is not a remote, mystic king who has failed some priestly test but a fallible man up-ended by his own zest for life. Kundry may appear a difficult character to read in the first two acts, with her schizophrenic activities and densely argued dialogue, but, be it as 'loathly damsel', seductress or penitent, her reactions throughout are thoroughly human. Klingsor's 'wonderful energy' (Debussy's phrase) is not something to feel ashamed of admiring — as some commentators seem to do, believing (perhaps) that Wagner gave the devil the best tunes by mistake. Like Karlheinz Stockhausen's Luzifer (in his *Licht* cycle), Klingsor is no conventional villain but a brilliant intellectual whose scientific experiments ideally leave no place for the 'crippled children' of humanity. He is *meant* to be energetic in contrast to the static Grail brethren: his energy, like science, is misused. This too is a human failing. Even Titurel's urgings to Amfortas have a direct rather than an abstract quality.

Wagner claimed that in using the Siegfried saga for his Nibelung dramas he was merely returning to *the* 'popular' German folk story. In *Parsifal*, beneath the layers of mysticism that have been foisted on it over the years, lies that drama of the people that he had always wanted to write.

Note. Nietzsche, and T.W. Adorno in his *Essay on Wagner*, had already made attacks on the 'dark' ideology of Wagner's last prose and musical works. They also discuss the composer's anti-semitism but to nothing like the exclusive degree of Hartmut Zelinsky, a Munich professor of German Studies, who, since the *Parsifal* centenary in 1982, has mounted a concentrated attack on Wagner in German newspapers, magazines and periodicals. See especially his 'review' of Martin Gregor-Dellin's Wagner biography and his essay 'Wie antisemitisch darf ein Künstler sein' (both in *Musik-Konzepte* magazine) and various articles for the *Süddeutsche Zeitung*, July/August 1982. The Rowohlt/Ricordi paperback on *Parsifal* (1984) gives a generous selection of excerpts from these writings — which deserve English translation. The American critic and author Robert W. Gut...an mounts a similar attack in his controversial biography, *Richard Wagner: The Man, His Mind and His Music*, a book that has (strangely) not been revised or updated since its first appearance in 1968. Replies to those two men have to date been weak and taken refuge in their (supposed) lack of knowledge of the musical score. Zelinsky has recently continued his attacks in Fonoforum Magazine, July/Septmber, 1985.

Recapitulation of a Lifetime

Dieter Borchmeyer

Wagner's last music drama was seventeen years in the making. He wrote the first prose draft towards the end of 1865. Twelve years later, during the early months of 1877, he drew up a second draft and the libretto. He began composing the music that same year and completed the full score on January 13, 1882. The work received its first performance in the Bayreuth Festspielhaus on July 26 of that year.

In almost every one of its characters and in the essential elements of its plot, *Parsifal* is a recapitulation, or what might be called a summation, of Wagner's *œuvre*. It is enough to read Cosima Wagner's diaries from the period during which Wagner was composing the music of *Parsifal* to note the remarkable frequency with which he related each of the characters of his 'last work' to the *dramatis personæ* of his earlier music dramas. A few examples will suffice.

In a conversation with Cosima on February 19, 1878, he asked, 'Who is Titurel?' His answer was: 'Wotan. After his renunciation of the world he is granted salvation, the greatest of possessions is entrusted to his care, and now he is guarding it like a militant god.' On March 2, 1878, a comparison suggested itself to him 'between Alberich and Klingsor'. Power at the cost of love and as revenge for its loss! — 'R. sees a resemblance between Wotan and Kundry', Cosima noted on June 4, 1878: 'both long for salvation and both rebel against it, Kundry in the scene with P., Wotan with Siegfried.' And on April 29, 1879 Wagner observed that 'in fact Siegfried ought to have turned into Parsifal and redeemed Wotan, he should have come upon Wotan (instead of Amfortas) in the course of his wanderings — but there was no antecedent for it, and so it would have to remain as it was.'

To a certain extent Parsifal is a more intense version of Siegfried; like the latter he is characterised by an erotic mother-complex, an 'inexperienced fool' and unthinking muscle man who soon renounces brute force and heroism. His breaking of his bow and throwing away his arrows is an act of purification whereby physical strength is spiritualised, and an ancient Germanic hero is transformed into a Christian anti-hero who learns what it is to suffer and whose very existence becomes a *passio* in the fullest sense of the word. Unlike Siegfried, who never attains to supreme 'knowledge' (this is reserved for the Norns' half-sister Brünnhilde) and who basically remains 'the stupid Siegfried' (to quote Nietzsche), Parsifal becomes worldly wise as a result of Kundry's kiss: made wise by pity, he ceases to be a fool.

As early as 1848, in his essay *The Wibelungs*, Wagner had associated the Grail with the Nibelung hoard. In the chapter headed 'The merging of the ideal content of the hoard with the "Holy Grail"', he had written: 'The quest for the Grail now replaces a striving after the Nibelung hoard', which is reduced to its 'real content' as 'an actual possession', 'ownership' or capital. 'Whereas, according to the oldest religious notions, the hoard appeared as the earth's splendour revealed to all by the light of day' — which is how the Rhinemaidens sing its praises — 'we later see it in condensed form as the hero's booty which gives him his power.' In other words, the Grail is the complement of the Nibelung's ring: whereas the Rhinegold, whose ideal and real meanings have not yet been divorced from each other, is reified as the ring

15

or 'a power-giving possession', the ideal content of the gold passes over into the 'anti-capital' of the Grail. This, then, is the extent of the relationship between *Parsifal* and *The Ring of the Nibelung*.

Clear links, however, can also be seen between Wagner's *Bühnenweih-festspiel* and almost all his other music dramas. As early as May 30, 1859, in a letter to Mathilde Wesendonck, Wagner called Amfortas 'my third-act Tristan infinitely intensified'. Bent upon dying, the king is reduced by the sight of the life-giving Grail to the same raging despair as that which Tristan is forced to suffer when, returning from the night of death, he is brought back to life by the power of the love potion. The reason why they die and the meaning of their deaths and, by analogy, the significance of the Grail and love potion are, of course, diametrically opposed to each other in the two works. Wagner originally planned to introduce Parsifal into the final act of *Tristan* as a stage in his quest for the Grail. Parsifal, who has felt within him 'the torment of love' as a result of his fellow-suffering with the tortured Amfortas — a fellow-suffering intensified to the point of self-suffering ('The wound, I saw it bleeding — / it's bleeding now in me') —, would have had a compassionate word to say about Tristan's 'terrible yearning'. Yet it would have been only 'sinful longing' for him, whereas Tristan lives beyond the categories of sin and purity, seeking salvation and redemption in the very love (of death) from which Parsifal would have had to cure and redeem him, just as he heals and redeems Kundry. Two worlds would have appeared here side by side, but without any link between them — which is yet another good reason why Wagner refrained from weaving Parsifal into the work.

There is a further work with which Parsifal's name is linked: *Lohengrin*. Here, of course, the Grail king has a son, who is none other than Lohengrin, since at the time when this Romantic Grail opera was written, Parsifal had heard of neither Schopenhauer nor the Buddha, and had therefore not yet wholly renounced erotic love. Only the name, but not the character, of the later Grail king is heralded here. Yet one can scarcely fail to notice that the Grail mysticism of *Parsifal* is related to *Lohengrin* (musically, too) and that, to a certain extent, the former is an intensified version of the latter. (Wagner's thoughts were revolving around the subject of Parsifal even as early as 1845, the period between the conception of *Tannhäuser* and *Lohengrin*.) But Wagner's final work also refers back to his other Romantic operas. Kundry is a female variant of the 'Wandering Jew', as Wagner himself noted in the 1865 prose draft. She is therefore the counterpart not only of the Flying Dutchman ('the Wandering Jew of the sea', as Heinrich Heine called him) but, at the same time, of Wotan, whom Wagner similarly described to Cosima as 'a kind of Flying Dutchman'.

Klingsor identifies Kundry as a reincarnation of Herodias ('Herodias were you'), who appears as the female counterpart of Ahasuerus in legends and poems from the Middle Ages onwards; like the Wandering Jew, she is condemned to a life of restless wanderings over the earth. Kundry, the Wandering Jewess, 'endlessly tormented through all existence', is therefore by no means a pure invention of Wagner's. The medieval myth was taken up again by Eugène Sue in his best-selling novel *Le juif errant* of 1844. Here Herodias accompanies Ahasuerus restlessly throughout history until, like Wagner's Kundry, she finds redemption. And there were other writers, too, who recast the medieval motif in the years around the middle of the nineteenth century. There is no doubt that Wagner was directly inspired by Heinrich Heine's *Atta Troll* of 1843 in his conception of Kundry. Here — as

16

Olive Fremstad as Kundry. She was a leading soprano at the Metropolitan Opera, New York, from 1903-1914 and was one of the great Isoldes and Brünnhildes of the century (photo: Metropolitan Opera Archives)

in many other nineteenth-century poems, including Mallarmé's *Hérodiade* — Herodias merges with her daughter Salome. Thus Wagner's Kundry is a reincarnation of both Herodias and Salome. As such, she has left behind her clearly definable traces in the poems of other *fin-de-siècle* authors, including Oscar Wilde and Villiers de l'Isle-Adam, both of whom wrote about Herodias/Salome. It is the curse of Ahasuerus and Kundry/Herodias that they must constantly repeat the very sin that was the reason for their having been cursed in the first place. In Nikolaus Lenau's ballad *The Wandering Jew* of 1839, we find the following strophe:

Weh mir, ich kann des Bilds mich nicht entschlagen,	Alas, the image haunts me evermore
Wie er um kurze Rast so flehend blickte,	Of how he begged to rest awhile, who came
Der Todesmüde, Schmach- und Schmerzgeknickte,	Aweary of this life, bowed down by shame
Muss ewig ihn von meiner Hütte jagen.	And grief, and whom I ordered from my door.

Just as Ahasuerus prevented Jesus from resting outside his door on the *via dolorosa*, so did Kundry laugh at Christ carrying the Cross. This is a radical reversal of the attitude which informs the metaphysical centre of *Parsifal*, namely elemental compassion for the suffering individual. That is why Kundry is forced to repeat her 'accursed laughter' with compulsive regularity, in addition to suffering the constraint of embodying time after time the depravity of Herodias/Salome.

It is in *Tannhäuser* (and above all in the Paris version of that opera), however, that the most striking parallels between *Parsifal* and any of Wagner's earlier works are to be found. Klingsor's *paradis artificiel* resembles the Venusberg; Kundry is a second Venus; and in both works the cave of wanton delights disappears at a stroke, in the one case at the sound of the blessed name of Maria or Mary, and, in the other, at the sign of the Cross. Tannhäuser experiences the same duality of heavenly and earthly love as does Parsifal, and is torn apart by the same conflict between erotic desire and an ascetic willingness to atone such as is felt by Amfortas. And just as Tannhäuser abandons the god-like status conferred upon him by erotic ecstasy in order to experience human suffering ('from joys I yearn to suffer anguish'), so Parsifal rejects, in a spirit of renunciation and for the sake of fellow-suffering, the supposed apotheosis promised him by the 'serpent of evil desire'.

In a letter to Ludwig II of September 7, 1865 (the year of the first prose draft), Wagner himself emphasised the connection between *Parsifal* and the Christian myth of the Fall as described in the Bible. In answer to the king's question, 'why does it take Kundry's kiss to convert our hero?', Wagner replied with an appeal to the mythology of paradise, the serpent and the tree of knowledge: 'After all, you know the serpent in paradise, and its beguiling promise: "eritis sicut Deus scientes bonum et malum" [Ye shall be as gods, knowing good and evil]. Adam and Eve became "knowing". They became "conscious of sin". The human race had to atone for that consciousness by suffering shame and misery, until redeemed by Christ who took upon himself the sins of the world.' In Kundry's kiss — that 'archetypal miss' as Wagner once described her to Cosima — we find a re-enactment of Eve's seduction of Adam, and in Amfortas's fall from grace Adam's original sin.

Alois Burgstaller as Parsifal at the Metropolitan Opera, where he was the first to sing the role in America, in 1903 (photo: Metropolitan Opera Archives)

Kundry is, as it were, the serpent of paradise. Just as Eve is promised that 'Ye shall be as gods', so, in the prose draft of 1865, we find Kundry inviting Parsifal to 'Enfold me now in love, and you will be God Himself this very day!' (In the final version of the libretto, this passage reads: 'The full embrace of my loving surely to godhead will raise you.') Original sin is therefore of an erotic sexual nature. Christ's act of redemption, in the context of Amfortas and Kundry, corresponds to Parsifal's act of salvation. Wagner's formula in his letter to the king reads: 'Adam — Eve: Christ. [. . .] Amfortas — Kundry: Parzival' (Wagner retained the medieval orthography of this name until March 1877.) As a result of Kundry's kiss Parsifal gains an awareness of sin that grants him entry to the race of those who 'know good and evil'. He who has not yet eaten of the fruit of the tree of knowledge knows nothing of good and evil until kissed by Kundry.

The analogy between Christ and Parsifal should be drawn only 'with a good deal of caution', Wagner stressed. He later opposed Hans von Wolzogen's view that Parsifal was a reflection of the Saviour: 'I didn't give the Redeemer a thought when I wrote it', he is said to have told Cosima on October 20, 1878. Wagner himself, then, clearly stated that he had never for a moment thought of regarding Parsifal as God or of making him a figure of redemption. There is not a single passage where a reference to the 'Redeemer' could mean anyone other than Christ. Parsifal is plainly conscious of the distance that separates him, as a sinner, from his Saviour: 'Redeemer! Saviour! Lord of Grace! Can I my sinful crime efface?' The closing formula, 'Redeemed the Redeemer', can in no sense be interpreted to mean that the new redeemer Parsifal has superseded the old one, in the way that each new Grail king replaces the previous one. If Parsifal participates in the redemptive acts of God, it is in the manner of a Christian saint, rescuing the Saviour, who is immanent within the Grail, from the guilt-tainted hands of Amfortas. This closing formula, which is in no sense enigmatic, in spite of speculative attempts to inflate its meaning, can be easily interpreted on the basis of the text itself, and specifically of the so-called 'Saviour's lament' in the second act: 'Redeem me, rescue me from hands defiled and guilty!'

Having placed himself in mortal hands in the shape of the Grail and having assumed material form as a sacred object which itself now stands apart from all action, Jesus needs a pure individual to redeem Him. This act of redemption is a *restitutio in integrum* which finds visual expression in the reunification of two objects that had become separated, namely the Spear and the Grail — the weapon which had wounded Jesus in the side and the vessel into which His blood had flowed. The ending marks the return to a beginning whose intensified recurrence is the restoration of a perfect primordial state. The blood that now flows from the Spear is no longer that of a sinner but of the Redeemer; Spear and Grail become a single entity in this sacred blood, and Amfortas's wound is healed when touched by the same Spear that had earlier caused it; the Grail fellowship is restored; Klingsor's alternative world is exorcised, and Nature returns to her paradisal innocence (Good Friday magic). It is a Christian Utopia which goes back to the late classical idea whereby all things are restored at the end of time.

Although the literary motifs and configurations of *Parsifal* bear a Christian stamp, there are of course other motivic groupings in which Hellenic myth repeatedly shines through. Parsifal, who heals Amfortas with the same Spear as had dealt the wound, relates back to Achilles, who healed Telephos in the same way, in accordance with the oracular pronouncement that 'He who dealt the wound shall heal it'. But Parsifal also resembles Heracles and his freeing of Prometheus, who similarly suffered a wound in his side that kept on tearing open. In the Christian tradition Prometheus has repeatedly been interpreted as a Christ-figure. Gerhart Hauptmann, for example, observed that 'the crucified Christ, with the open wound in his breast, looks very much like

20

Lillian Nordica, the first American artist to be engaged at Bayreuth, as Kundry (photo: Metropolitan Opera Archives)

Heinrich Hensel, the first London Parsifal, at Covent Garden in 1914 (Royal Opera House Archives)

Prometheus bound to his rock'. Because Jesus's wound was dealt Him by Longinus's spear, the very weapon with which Klingsor wounded Amfortas, the latter's wound becomes an *imitatio perversa* of the Saviour's wound. Greek myth and Christian legend are interlinked here in an intimate typological nexus.

Wagner reserved his *Bühnenweihfestspiel* exclusively for the Bayreuth Festival, and this demonstrates the seriousness with which he regarded the religious form and content of his final music drama. In the face of the fossilisation and denominational disputes of contemporary Christianity, he believed that art might rescue 'true religion', a point which he advances programmatically in his 1880 essay *Religion and Art*. It is reserved to art, we read here, 'to salvage the kernel of religion, inasmuch as the mythical images which religion would wish to be believed as true are apprehended in art for their symbolic value, and through ideal representation of those symbols art reveals the concealed deep truth within them.'

The foregoing article is based upon the author's *Das Theater Richard Wagners: Idee Dichtung — Wirkung*, published by Reclam-Verlag, Stuttgart, in 1982. An English translation of this book is planned for 1987.

The extracts from *Cosima Wagner's Diaries*, edited and annotated by Martin Gregor-Dellin and Dietrich Mack, translated and with an introduction by Geoffrey Skelton, New York/London 1978-80, are reproduced by kind permission of the publishers, Messrs. William Collins Sons & Co Ltd, London and Harcourt Brace Jovanovich Inc, New York.

Experiencing Music and Imagery in 'Parsifal'

Robin Holloway

Parsifal is the supreme instance of music-drama realised by means of a sonorous image-cluster: a central complex of metaphor expresses at once the story and the characters whose story it is; and the broader subject-matter that lies within character and event; all this is caught or borne by the music, everything fusing together into an indivisible whole. There is nothing like it in any other composer; indeed the only comparison is with the relationship of plot and character with verbal imagery in mature Shakespearian tragedy.

The sonorous image-cluster grows from the directer though not necessarily simple leitmotivic usage in *The Ring**. It is special to *Tristan* and *Parsifal* and can more easily be described in the earlier work. All the central material in *Tristan* is manifestly related to the melody, chord, progression, of the opening. Its unmissable recurrences, carefully placed at hinges in the story which are also crucial in expression both of subject and psychological theme, project local meaning into large-scale aural architecture. For each further reference to the opening recalls and includes those before, requiring the listener to remember and compare, to make intelligible and therefore to interpret, its ever-wider-ramifying implications. The opening also generates endless detail that gradually aligns itself and merges with material at first apparently quite distinct. And so it can eventually gather together the whole enormous span, being at once its outer limits, its principal junctions, and its core. It is not a leitmotif; its use is far too rich and pervasive to be named. It is all-comprehending — what the work is made of and what it is about. The sonorous image-cluster is the nucleus that gives life to the work's expressive and musical substance.

This, together with the altogether different *Mastersingers* technique of building huge diatonic paragraphs that unfold quasi-polyphonically on a minimum of leitmotivic material, is *Parsifal*'s starting point. In some ways it is simpler, as if after the overwhelming abundance and complexity of the last four acts of *The Ring* Wagner is not so much returning to basics (though there is an element of this) as refining and quintessentialising all his discoveries, concentrated in a chalice rather than spilling forth from a cornucopia. Indeed this final simplicity can sometimes seem calculated to *demonstrate*, as well as to explore, a close area of tight interconnections. Every character in *Parsifal* can be identified by a thematic tag as if we were back in *Rhinegold*. Hearing a major triad with added sixth (i), or a minor triad with strong augmented coloration (ii):

(i)   (ii)

we know at once who is meant and how they are related. Have the minor triad rise rather than fall, diminish then expand its fifth, and a whole physiognomy and psychology come instantly to mind (iii). Take the same phrase but lower the

---

* See the introductory paragraphs of this writer's essay in the ENO/ROH Opera Guide to *Twilight of the Gods*.

Jon Vickers as Parsifal at Covent Garden in 1971 (photo: Donald Southern)

octave from the third note and continue in sequence (iv) and we have an equally recognisable character, related significantly to the one before.

(iii)   (iv)

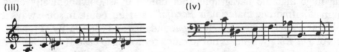

Such demonstrativeness might seem like a reversion to the earliest phase of leitmotivic technique. But *Tristan* has intervened, where the lovers are merged into the central sonorous image to such a point of cross-identity (even interchangeability) as neither to possess, or need, individual themes. And what is new to *Parsifal* is the small differentiation of the character-tags. The motifs just shown are for the four principal characters — Parsifal, Amfortas, Kundry, Klingsor — but what they have in common is as important as what makes them distinct.

Their common ground lies ultimately in their relation to the six-bar melody whose quadruple statement so unforgettably opens the entire work. First it comes in the major [1] in subtly-scored unison, and is at once reiterated surrounded by a fleecy nimbus of repeated chords and arpeggios, trailing off into the heights. After a long pause the melody returns in the minor, rhythmically, intervallically and orchestrally intensified; again the fully-scored and harmonised presentation follows and disappears into silence. This wonderfully fertile melodic shape, in its diatonic and chromatic versions, gathers in or gives out all the central material of the work. In the major mode it is sometimes used complete, as during Communion in Act One, and can be broadened into the sweeping melodic arcs of the choruses that follow. All the motifs bracketed within [1] are in play throughout (the version of (a) reserved for two moments of special fulfilment is important enough to be called [2]). And this major-mode version also contains the multitude of simple diatonic fragments that make up the work's imagery of goodness, innocence, holiness, purity in nature and in the human heart — from the Dresden Amen [25], the motifs of dove [11], swan [22] and Monsalvat bells [30], to the music of Nature's healing in Act One [40] and its full flowering in the Good Friday baptism [27] and meadows [28] in Act Three, from the most gigantic diatonic sound in the whole work, the long-sustained alternations of tonic and dominant in the whole orchestra when Parsifal is crowned Lord of the Grail, to the serene terraces of consonance upon which it closes.

All these interconnections are summarised in the following slightly tongue-in-cheek ideogram (which puts all the music into the work's opening and closing key of A b for ease of comparison). It can be read left to right for musical line and story-line; and up and down for the vertical parallels that support the sense one has when listening that all this material is made out of the same diatonic shapes.

25

The minor-mode or chromatic version of the opening melody is more a source from which grows, rather than a synthesis of, the work's imagery of guilt, suffering, and the uncleanness that yearns for purification and redemption:

Amfortas's theme is made from (x) inverted followed by (y) the right way up (given here in C and simplified to facilitate comparison):

Kundry's theme [4] derives from a conflation of the first bar with the chromatic intensification of the second; while the dissonant harmony associated with her uncouth laughter is taken from the crucial chord in Amfortas's theme (its third bar), spelling out by sonorous means the connection that binds them. Klingsor's theme [7] is a further filling-out of the Kundry-shape (as shown more simply in the third paragraph, above); and many other chromatic motifs and fragments associated with guilt and suffering derive from the same fertile six bars of the prelude.

The major and minor versions of this passage, taken together, focus the sense that the whole enormous work is mainly made out of a surprisingly small web of closely-related motifs not very greatly distinct from each other. This would seem to make the central core a contrast, or series of connected contrasts, set up in the basic musical material itself, which embodies those in the story and its characters: between purity and impurity, innocence (or 'foolishness') and guilt, chastity and carnality, spiritual health and spiritual sickness, selfless compassionate suffering for others and suffering that indulges its torment in remorse and self-pity. Not that these contrasts are peripheral, and that their presentation is in any way muted. I have rather diagrammatically indicated their raw musical constituents; in the opera itself they are rendered with an immediacy that raises psychological excruciation to a pitch unlikely to be surpassed on this scale. But beyond this it is Wagner's extraordinary achievement in *Parsifal* to show the oppositions that apparently make up his very subject-matter to be deeply interfused and interdependent, utterly ambiguous, in the end not opposed after all. From this fusion at the centre, and the sonorous imagery that embodies it in music, spring story and character, music and meaning, reaching outwards to the work's extremes of differentiation. The nucleus is more than a dynamic equilibrium of tensions; it is reconciliation and accord.

On a straightforward level the apparent opposites begin to meet and mingle from the very start of Gurnemanz's narration. These early stages of Act One, sometimes held to be monotonous even by those who admire *Parsifal* 'once it gets going', seem to me one of the summits of Wagner's art (all the more so for being so little a setpiece), unrolling with a casualness that conceals the utmost mastery all the prior events and all the thematic relationships that will be needed to follow action and music when they advance into the present.

Alexander Kipnis as Gurnemanz, a role in which he was particularly admired at Covent Garden, where he sang between 1929 and 1935 (Royal Opera House Archives)

After the vast diatonic spaces evoked by the prelude and, when the curtain rises, the still more motionless morning prayer that seems to close the work before it has begun, comes the first intimation (as Gurnemanz falls into his narrative) of Amfortas and his never-ceasing pain [45], and a hint of the prophecy of the innocent fool who will heal it [54]. The first flicker of faster music, describing Kundry's wild ride, is built out of her driving ostinato rhythm [5] and culminates in the piercing discord and plunging descent of her laughter [36]. This temporary momentum and volume collapse into soft stasis as in exhaustion she delivers the balsam to ease the man whose suffering she has caused. (So far, then, vast diatonic calm with little scuds and flurries of the disturbances to come.) Amfortas is borne in on his litter, and the earlier intimations of his music grow into a big slow paragraph combining the chromatic music of his pain-racked exhaustion with the pentatonic evocation of the waters that might quench it [40]. He takes further the hint of a prophesied deliverance, but it still remains incomplete and he equates its fulfilment with death. Enquiring the origin of the balsam he actually talks with Kundry, thus bringing his music of pain into proximity with her painful laughter as she spurns his thanks and hurries him off to temporary assuagement, for which the pentatonic strains take over again. (Does Amfortas know who she is and how he encountered her before? Gurnemanz obviously does not; and Kundry obviously *does* — her silent presence throughout this exposition, being who she is, having done what she has done, is a powerful part of its total effect.)

The Wolfgang Wagner production at Bayreuth in 1980: Gurnemanz berates Parsifal for killing a swan on sanctified ground (photo: Festspielleitung Bayreuth)

Amfortas (Tom Krause) uncovers the Grail in Act One of the 1982 Geneva production while Parsifal (Siegfried Jerusalem), Gurnemanz (Peter Meven) and the Grail Knights look on (photo: Grand Théâtre de Genève)

The young squires talk ill of her as she lies on the ground like a troubled beast. Gurnemanz's sober reproof uses only what of hers we have heard already, the driving rhythm and the laughter, to describe further her paradoxical impulses of humility and hatred. Their querulousness subsides into questioning: by now a sufficient base of information has been unobtrusively divulged for him to embark on the almost casual reminiscences that their questions elicit. And only now, as he describes how Titurel found her in deathly sleep when the castle of the Grail was built, do we hear her actual motif for the first time [4]. The narration alludes in passing to 'the evil one over the mountains', neither naming him nor giving him his theme. Kundry's contact with him is still as unknown to us as it will forever remain to Gurnemanz, which makes an unbearable irony when he addresses her direct — 'Where were *you* then / When by our Lord the spear was lost?' (to a full exposition of her theme, together with the chord and plunge of her laughter).

First mention of the spear and its loss signals a return to fragments of motif from the opening melody of the prelude. As the tale turns towards Amfortas and his fall the now completely familiar Kundry-theme is much in evidence: listening, we make the connection that is painfully well-known to one person on stage — if not at the first time of hearing, then (with hindsight) at every subsequent one. Gurnemanz's description of the fatal far distant kiss casts a long look forward towards the kiss we will actually witness in Act Two, upon which the entire story and music are centred. Both kisses are made with a powerful pun by which the upward semitone in Kundry's motif is dwelt upon, intensified, and transformed into the motif from bars 2-3 of the opening melody:

Fleshly pleasure audibly turns to fleshly anguish as, at the moment of delight, Klingsor (now named for the first time) seized the spear from its neglectful guardian, pierced his side and escaped with it, laughing.

The evil one's name is dropped rapidly and in passing. The third squire catches it and uses it to prompt the old man into more story. But here the present impinges again; Amfortas's litter bears him back from lake to castle; as it passes offstage the music of sickness and healing is briefly encapsulated. Our interest, caught before because we saw him and because the music carried such a weight of unexplained suffering, is now heightened by the narrative's interruption at such a point, even though we do not now see him. Gurnemanz, after asking how the King fares, falls into sad brooding over the past. But the third boy insists upon knowing about Klingsor. The answer is at first oblique, consisting instead of an account of something still further back, Titurel's vision that led to the erection of the sanctuary to guard the sacred relics, spear and chalice, and the foundation of the Knighthood of the Grail. This is set to an enormous paragraph interwoven à la *Mastersingers* out of the Dresden Amen ([25] — hitherto always separated from the musical flow and, anyway, not heard since the offstage brass that extended the prelude beyond its ending into the stillness of the morning prayer), the opening melody, and the chorale-like music that evokes the vision [14]. Only after this, the most continuous movement heard since the curtain rose, makes a full Amen-close, does Gurnemanz get round to answering. (We learn to enjoy the affection as

Set Svanholm, the Swedish tenor, as Parsifal (photo: Metropolitan Opera Archives)

well as the art which employs throughout the whole narration an old man's dogged slowness that gets around to everything eventually, but in its own good time.) Now, as he tells fully the story of Klingsor, the moment has at last come to hear his motif [7]. We learn of his longing to achieve holiness; how it was denied him because he could not deaden his lusts; his drastic self-mutilation that gained mastery over magical powers able to win what his failed sanctity never could, lordship of the relics; of the perfumed garden of earthly delights (again a vignette of forepleasure that will blossom for us in full actuality as an intermezzo on the journey towards the kiss that has been already anticipated); of Amfortas's expedition, armed with the spear, to raze the evil place over the mountains.

What there became of it and him has already been recounted; the narration peters out in gloomy inconclusion. But we are nearly up-to-date, and this (Gurnemanz continues) is how things stand: Klingsor holds the spear and the means to seduce the guardian knights into gaining him the Grail too. (Kundry listens to all this mingling of sacred and profane in a writhing fury of agitation.) The deadlock is illustrated with a full exposure of Klingsor's motif. But a gleam of hope survives in another vision, vouchsafed to the guilty lord himself, and built upon the 'Amen', at first in tortuous chromatic distortions that clarify into complete diatonic purity for the return of the opening melody (major mode) with a beautiful enharmonic change on its climactic note. The prophecy of the chaste fool made wise by pity, twice hinted at, is now repeated by Gurnemanz with its hitherto unheard second half ([54] — which only comes complete in one other place, at the end of Amfortas's monologue just before the Grail is revealed and the sacraments consecrated). Its already-known first half is taken up by the four squires; the pregnant stillness is interrupted by cries of outrage, the flight of the wounded swan, and the precipitate entry of the prophecy's unlikely embodiment, not named for a long time yet and not recognised for far longer, though his motif rings out brave and clear. And so the action of the opera begins.

This remarkable exposition has presented the work's opposite musical poles in subtle alternation and shown them to be, at least, highly interdependent. But the nucleus where opposites are fused has still not been reached. It comes in the extraordinary sound that summons up *Parsifal* to anyone who has ever heard it, as surely as *Tristan* is summoned up by its opening bars — the work's central sonorous image as heard thrice in the transformation-music that shifts the scene from forest exterior to the interior of the sanctuary:

This music is not even thematic, let alone leitmotivic. It comes as a slab of orchestral texture, of processional movement, of harmonic suspension, that puts the bowels into heat. Or, technically speaking, it is simply a segment of sequence, indefinitely extensible and indestructible and useful — musical material in the abstract, like something baroque.* It is baroque also in its *Affekt* — a conventional icon of weeping and sighing, weighed down with grief, thrust against a mighty bass that bears its load gladly and if not checked will pound on for ever round the cycle of fifths. Together these two functions produce the central sonorous image of *Parsifal*: the baroque *Affekt* that burns expression into sound, making a symbol actual, that then gathers up ever more resonance by altered contexts and further associations until it achieves a satiety of expressive utterance: while the baroque usefulness of this sturdy material that can do anything and go anywhere provides a norm of continuity and cadence that can be extended all the way from local frisson to large-scale structure. The combination is powerful enough to carry the complex and contradictory meaning of the whole work.

Here is how this overwhelmingly plangent final result grows, via a few hypothetical intervening stages, from the opening melody. Its minor version (see page 26) placed a new emphasis on the penultimate bar — it is sharper in rhythm and more dynamic in volume, being turned towards a second climax on the low B♮ rather than the dying away of the major mode version. It is this penultimate bar that contains the seed of the sound that surfaces in the transformation music. The major version, in A♭, ended on its third, C; the chromatic version, in C minor, ends on its tonic, C; the sense implicit even in this unharmonised line that the last bar might, after all, cadence into A♭

is the kernel. This coloration of an interrupted cadence where both bass and third move up a semitone to resolve, but not together, making a rich major-minor poignancy, becomes the norm of resolution for the whole work.

It has already been fully discovered in the closing stages of the prelude, where a series of sequences grows from the expiring end of the opening melody in a pattern whose prototype might be

* Compare two places in Contrapunctus XI from *The Art of Fugue* where, known to Wagner or not, Bach has hit upon the same sonority and sequence — bars 118-9 and more particularly 142-5.

Three possible stages in its growth towards full complexity might be

— though of course there is nothing so formulaic as these, and what Wagner
actually *does* do towards the close of the prelude, and then in the earlier stages
of the transformation music before this material reveals its full power, is
worth looking at with these crude prototypes in mind.

The surest way to give meaning to this music that works above all by
intense unspecificness, is to take it first at its most explicit and then follow it
back and forward into the different contexts that extend its range. It breaks
out with Amfortas's words when, the company assembled, Titurel asks to see
the Grail again before he dies. Guilt and suffering are the keywords here; at its
next appearance Amfortas tells of the 'unequalled punishment borne by the
tormented Lord of mercy'; and at its next, of the spear that 'inflicted the
sacred wound / Through which with bleeding tears / The Holy One wept for
the sins of man / In pity's holiest yearning.' This sound can thus conflate
Amfortas's pain-racked guilt with Christ's guiltless agony. That it is not just
private to Amfortas we have already heard when the knights' procession used
the same music in turning from solemn festive diatonicism over the bells'
ostinato, to allude to the Redeemer's blood-sacrifice for sinful mankind. This
in turn is a mere echo of its huge use in the triple climax of the transformation
where sinful mankind *en masse* treads the same sequential steps weighed
down with the same groaning burden.

Later, as the Eucharist is celebrated despite Amfortas's attempts to stop it
('How radiant God's greeting today!' — another instance of Wagner's
grandiose slow-motion irony), the sonorous image returns in a mystic
shimmer as of sexuality transfigured into spirituality, which while still
echoing its intensest and most visceral usages (all of them heard by Parsifal
himself), takes us back to the final stages of the prelude (as the Communion
itself had repeated its four-fold opening) where the sonority first grew into
being. After the distribution of bread and wine the knights process
diatonically from the hall, cleansed by the ceremony, leaving the disturbing
music behind with Parsifal. Here it renders his puzzled incomprehension:
Amfortas's suffering, and everything it contains, is refracted through

Klingsor's castle in the 1973 Munich production by Dietrich Haugk, designed by Günther Schneider-Siemssen with costumes by Bernd Müller and Jörg Neumann (photo: Anne Kirchbach)

Parsifal's ignorant and unconscious identification with it. When the sanctuary is empty save for the old man and the young fool, pure C-major is reached, rudely interrupted by another use for the image, to accompany Parsifal's wordless answer (he can only repeat the convulsive clutch of hand over heart that first seized him when hearing Amfortas cry for mercy) to Gurnemanz's ill-humoured cross-examination. After Gurnemanz pushes him out as a goose the soft repetition of the prophecy tells us again that this is indeed the long-desired swan, and the music resumes its celestial C-major with chorus and bells, in which the interruption seems scarcely to have happened.

From this catalogue of its occurrences in Act One we realise that the crucial sonorous image of *Parsifal* is quite different from its equivalent in *Tristan*. There it is the first, unforgettable music we hear, returning unmistakably at all the crucial places, and sublimely resolving at the end. In *Parsifal* the nucleus slowly comes into being; it has to be uncovered and found; though all-permeating it can disappear for long stretches, and its eventual course is gradual assuagement and elimination rather than a grand final integration. In Act Two its increased versatility allows it to encompass and connect more and more meaning. It produces at the climax of the prelude an obscene parody of the Act One transformation for the comparable entry into Klingsor's anti-Grail castle, showing his impotent mockery of holiness to be imbued with a suffering of its own. In another guise it accompanies Kundry's ascent into wakefulness from the timeless void she inhabits when between two worlds; it accompanies her moan of 'Sehnen' ('longing') that Klingsor can only interpret sardonically. A little later she tells us, to the same strains, what it is she longs for — sleep, release, salvation. Her longing is already tinged with eroticism, for Klingsor has now galvanised her almost completely into her other role, at first unwilling, then avidly, pitifully compliant, as seductress. Far further on, after the seduction has failed, her explanation to her victim-victor of *why* she longs for sleep and release, the laughter at Christ on his cross that condemns her to wander the earth's surface down the centuries in crazed hilarity, is again set to the same musical image.

And, of course, it permeates Parsifal's outburst immediately after the kiss, realising its full baroque potential in a modern re-creation of the ritornello, the one stable element in the astonishing *mélange* of motifs that accompany his astonishing words (in bold where it is used).

PARSIFAL

Amfortas!	Amfortas!
The Spear-wound! — The Spear-wound! —	Die Wunde! — Die Wunde! —
It burns here in my heart!	Sie brennt in meinem Herzen!
Oh! Torment! Torment!	**Oh! Klage! Klage!**
Fearfullest torment,	**Furchtbare Klage,**
the cry of anguish pierces my heart.	**aus tiefstem Herzen schreit sie mir auf.**
Oh! — Oh! —	**Oh! — Oh! —**
Keen anguish!	**Elender!**
Piteous sufferer!	**Jammervollster!**
The wound that I saw bleeding	Die Wunde seh ich bluten,
is bleeding now **in me!**	nun blutet sie **in mir!**
Here — here!	**Hier — hier!**
No! No! Not the Spear-wound is it.	Nein! Nein! Nicht die Wunde ist es.
Freely the blood may stream from my side!	Fliesse ihr Blut in Strömen dahin!
Here, a flame in my heart!	Hier, im Herzen der Brand!
The yearning, the wild fearful yearning	Das Sehnen, das furchtbare Sehnen,
that fills my senses and holds them fast!	das alle Sinne mir fasst und zwingt!
Oh! — pain of loving!	**Oh! — Qual der Liebe!**
How all things tremble, quiver and shake	Wie Alles schauert, bebt und zuckt
in sinful, guilty yearning!	in sündigem Verlangen!

While Kundry stares at him in fear and wonder, Parsifal appears to fall wholly into a trance. He continues calmly.

This gaze is fixed now on the holy Cup —	Es starrt der Blick dumpf auf das Heilsgefäss —
The sacred blood now glows:	Das heil'ge Blut erglüht:
redemption's rapture, sweet and mild,	**Erlösungswonne, göttlich mild,**
To every heart brings all its healing:	**durchzittert weithin alle Seelen:**
but here — in this heart will the pain not lessen.	nur hier — im Herzen will die Qual nicht weichen.
The Saviour's cry is stealing through me,	**Des Heilands Klage da vernehm' ich,**
lamenting, ah, lamenting	**die Klage, ach die Klage**
for the profaned sanctuary:	**um das entweih'te heiligtum:**
"Redeem me, rescue me	"Erlöse, rette mich
from hands defiled and guilty!"	aus schuldbefleckten Händen!"
Thus rang his lamentation,	So rief die Gotteslage
fearful, **loud, loud to my spirit.**	furchtbar **laut mir in die Seele.**
And I, a fool, a coward,	Und ich — der Tor, der Feige,
to childish deeds of daring fled away!	zu wilden Knabenthaten floh ich hin!

He throws himself despairingly on his knees.

Redeemer! Saviour! Lord of grace!	**Erlöser! Heiland! Herr der Huld!**
Can I my sinful crime efface?	**Wie büss ich Sünder meine Schuld?**

Franz Mazura as Klingsor and Yvonne Minton as Kundry in the 1982 Geneva production by Rolf Liebermann, designed by Petrika Ionesco and Bernard Daydé (photo: Grand Théâtre de Genève)

Anton Fuchs as Klingsor at Bayreuth in 1882 (Royal Opera House Archives)

In Act Three, fitting the trajectory of the work as a whole, this central musical image is distanced; though what it represents is still unassuaged, its recurrences seem to echo from a remote past. Its overlapping interrupted cadences are first heard again as the mysterious black-armoured knight approaches, and is given its most beautiful treatment of all when Gurnemanz eventually recognises him and the spear he carries; the descending major thirds follow at once as, at the height of the pious old man's exaltation, Kundry is compelled to avert her gaze from what she recognises all-too-poignantly. It thrice shadows the Good Friday meadows as a brief reminder of sin and suffering long ago. The pastoral episode first emerges from its decline after Kundry is baptised; it returns as Gurnemanz tells of the Cross that this day perpetually memorialises (she was there), then recedes as he tells of the purification of nature effected by Christ's sacrifice; and is heard again at the pastoral's close, when Parsifal juxtaposes magic flowers of evil with natural flowers of good, chastely returns Kundry's kiss and absolves her of her curse — a ghost of what had once been the most powerful noise in the opera, soon to be succeeded by sounds from the still-remoter past, the Monsalvat bells stealing across the meadows, not heard since Act One.

It remains ghost-like in Amfortas's second monologue; after the huge impact of the second transformation-music and the communal outcry against him, it barely flickers into life just before his first words of exhausted sorrow. It is heard for the last time as the 'pure fool made wise by pity' touches the racked body of his predecessor and reunites spear with chalice: 'This holy weapon that has healed you / Upon its point fresh blood is flowing / And yearning to join the kindred fountain / That darkly in the Grail is glowing'.

So the central sonorous image in *Parsifal* is a sort of virus, that contaminates everything it touches, sates itself, and works its way out — more like a far more complex and loaded version of the curse-motif in *The Ring* than the progression in *Tristan*, whose goal is its integration into the work's final cadence. And its use is so wide-ranging that what it eventually stands for would seem to be uncontainably contradictory. Its ubiquity and omni-purposefulness indicate more than the fusion of opposites; they show the fusion to express an experience of communal rather than individual import. The characters overlap; each is a version of the other, undergoing the same trial according to his lights. If the words and story are considered in isolation, this is explicit to the point of formula (which excites the pleasure of symbolists, allegorists and symmetry-lovers, and the disapproval of those who find such things manipulated and frigid). It is obvious that Klingsor is a spoilt Amfortas; that Klingsor's self-willed abstention mirrors Parsifal's involuntary temptation and restraint; that Parsifal re-lives Amfortas's adventure but emerges unscathed; and that Kundry is the unchanging instrument of their various progresses. But, as always with Wagner, it is the musical realisation of such symmetries that saves them from stiffness, making them not merely more intelligible and interesting, but flexible, significant, profound beyond the power of unaided words. This is why these four principal characters' individuating motifs are less important than their interrelationship and common origin in the work's opening theme. This is why the work's central sonority, also growing out of the opening theme, impartially expresses them all, melting black/white, good/bad, diatonic/chromatic, into a fermenting elixir where truth resides, for all that the formal layout of the story itself, from the largest massing to the smallest details, is built around these stark polarities.*

The clearest indication that the principal characters overlap is the music of their main monologues. These are all fashioned from the same ingredients, and the identifying motifs, which in *The Ring* would be paramount, are scarcely present. To be sure, Amfortas's Act One monologue begins aria-like with his motif in the orchestra, to which he then sings his first two lines of verse. But thereafter his own music is present in just two references, lasting four bars in all, to the augmented-triad motif that represented his pain as he was borne to the waters of the lake. The monologue is otherwise made of many contradictory motifs writhed together in desperate *mélange* — the Amen and the opening melody, Kundry's motif and Klingsor's that grows out of it, the dissonance and plunging descent of her laughter, and the ubiquitous ritornello of the basic sonorous image. In Klingsor's briefer passage of self-expression in the first scene of Act Two the first two lines are again sung to his own musical contour (though it is also Kundry's) and the rest is the mixture as before: Amfortas's augmented-triad is used more here than by Amfortas himself, Kundry's laughter is given the spitting orchestral sharpness unique to this scene, one Amen is well-aimed at a dissonant rather than consonant climax, and the whole is framed by the basic sonority.

Parsifal's outburst upon being kissed uses neither his motif nor the prophecy that pertains to him. The kiss itself begins as an exact replica (though more solemnly prepared, richly-scored, and lingered-over) of the kiss between Kundry and Amfortas already described by Gurnemanz in Act One. But it goes horribly wrong. The memory of Amfortas's guilty agony comes between the youth and the woman, he clutches his heart as twice before and

* The best symmetrical chart of the opera is Wieland Wagner's *Parsifal-Cross*.

cries out the unforgotten name to an intensification of the unforgettable cry for mercy. Thereafter the music is a still wilder *mélange* of exactly the same ingredients again, thrown together in a rush of free-association that defies grammatical analysis even while it captures a psychological reaction with horrifying precision and the utmost intensity. At the end of Act One he had been dumbstruck and incomprehending like a fool. Before, we had seen his first uncouth actions, his bashful gormlessness about his name and origins, and his dangerous vulnerability over his mother. And we have followed almost every step in his action since, from the boyish love of wild adventure that has brought him to Klingsor's castle, and bloody encounter with Klingsor's knights (described by their master from his ramparts), to amorous encounter with Klingsor's girls (as enjoyed in sight and sound on stage) and seduction above and below the belt by a Kundry now young, beautiful and calling him by the name his mother once used. As she kisses him all this experience fuses: Wagner's power to yoke opposites in powerful symbiosis is never more daring than his hero's substitution of a burning in his side after such build-up to a burning somewhere else. The conflation of sexual excitement kindled by Kundry with the guilty compunction she had aroused for his mother's death produces a total identification with Amfortas and his torment. It is presented in an inextricable tangling of opposites — base and exalted, carnal and spiritual, painful and pleasurable* — that fuse into one overwhelming meaning-fused sound.

It is overwhelming also because we have been through it before and know its every element. All the music for the central characters' crucial places is made from the same cluster of motifs. It is a game with three chances. By the time Parsifal's turn comes round it is ours too. His version of the experience is incomparably more protracted and intensive than his predecessors'; it is indeed the main event in the opera. Every sign has indicated him to be the one who does not fail where the others failed, who breaks the pattern. But though he is clearly from the start the chosen one, he is not distinct and individual. As the music shows, he is a generality, a composite of his predecessors and a representative man, elected to carry our burden and undergo initiation into an understanding that connects and integrates high and low.

*   *   *

Parsifal the character may be of necessity something of an identikit or cut-out figure. *Parsifal* the opera is anything but; it is indeed quite unique. At its centre is an excruciatingly vivid exploration of the blackest and bloodiest places of carnal psychopathology and their intimate connection with every aspect of the personality. This is caught and expressed in the physical and psychological power of the work's sonorous imagery, fusing its subject and meaning into the musical materials from which it is made. This red-hot central matter burns its way out of the work; assuaged and eventually rendered harmless, it completely disappears. And in doing so, it puts right old wrongs; the goal of the work is restoration, refreshment, revivication.

So the *Bühnenweihfestspiel* is not so much an allegory of Everyman, nor a Passion-play, as a rite of purification. It is presented as something of gigantic significance and elevation, absolutely not normal or realistic. No one could

---

* He has not forgotten Amfortas's words, nor their music, that he heard in Act One, when 'transfixed by rapturous and joyful pain' at the flow of sacred blood from Jesus's side and the sullied blood from his own.

exactly call it a comedy — and there is certainly no double-wedding in sight at the end, nor any intimation of generation even at Tamino-level (let alone Papageno!) — yet the sense as the prophecy is fulfilled, the spear touches the wound and rejoins the chalice, and the music settles down into A*b*, is very much that of 'happy ever after'.

Perhaps the work *is* best understood as a super-charged fairy-tale. Klingsor, Amfortas and Parsifal — they are like the three wishes where only the third, restoring the *status quo ante*, gets it right; or the three sons, where only the youngest is wily (in this case dumb) enough to avoid his elders' mistakes and win the girl (in this case Grail). This is not so silly as it sounds. Concentration upon the liturgical element and the perfervid language of guilt and redemption that has from the start provoked on the one hand such derision and on the other such misplaced religiosity, tends to direct the communal hero along a *via dolorosa* or at least a pilgrim's progress. But a truer parallel is with Wagner's previous hero Siegfried. It would be interesting and illuminating to open up the comparison between his pagan and his Christian paragons; for all the immense difference of context, manner, story and imagery, there is more in common between them than there is separation; and the principal adventure for both lies in their discovering who they are, and what they can do about it.

The Temple of the Holy Grail at the Salzburg Festival in the production by Herbert von Karajan, designed by Günther Schneider-Siemssen, 1981 (photo: Siegfried Lauterwasser)

In Syberberg's film of 'Parsifal' (1982), the action takes place on a vast model of Wagner's death mask. Here, the Good Friday meadows of Act Three are spread beneath his nostrils. Parsifal is played alternately by Karin Krick (above) and Michael Kutter, and sung by Reiner Goldberg; Kundry acted by Edith Clever and sung by Yvonne Minton; Gurnemanz by Robert Lloyd (photo: Artificial Eye)

'Parsifal': Words and Music

Carolyn Abbate

'One of the most beautiful edifices in sound ever raised to the glory of music': so Debussy paid homage to *Parsifal* in 1903.[1] But if we pause to reflect on his words, we see that his praise is double-edged, and his adoration touched with ambiguity. 'Edifice in sound' evokes an architectural image of the score, an image of notes, melodic shape, harmony, all spun into some sonic edifice. At the same time, the phrase turns its back on another part of *Parsifal*, its dramatic and poetic existence as libretto. To be sure, this is a sanctioned slight. While few would deny the mastery Wagner displays in every bar of the score, many would prefer to forget the cloying Christian myth-making that permeates the dramatic conceit or the infelicities in the poem. Arnold Whittall has written of the opera as a 'tonal work of art' whose hallmark is a 'resourceful manipulation of [musical] material to build satisfying, coherent structures',[2] musical structures that have nothing in particular to do with plot or characters. The idea that Wagner's drama resides in his music, and in an abstract form-building interplay of motif and tonality, is deeply embedded in our histories of 19th- and 20th- century music. We have refashioned Wagner in Beethoven's image, as a composer of pure music. This image of Wagner is, of course, revealed to be illusion, if we look closely at the connections between poetry and music in *The Ring*, or even in *Tristan*. Wagner's musical imagination was frequently stimulated by words, and his music shaped by them. *Parsifal* may seem the most abstract or symphonic of Wagner's scores because the orchestral preludes and interludes are given such tremendous prominence and temporal weight. But Wagner had not, in this last work, lost his lifelong fascination with musical metaphors. He brought to bear on *Parsifal* his accumulated experience as a composer of music for poetry and for the stage, from the leitmotivic games played in *Rhinegold*, through the scene-structuring experiments of *Valkyrie* and *Siegfried*, to the harmonic symbolism of *Tristan* and the allegorical motivic transformations in *Twilight of the Gods*. In this most concentrated and 'abstract' of Wagner's scores, not only music but the union of music and language are treated with an intensity unmatched in any other work.

* * *

If the music of *Parsifal* is among Wagner's most introverted, relying as it does upon the smaller gesture and the subtler transformation, the structure of the drama declares itself in less equivocal terms. The three acts form an arch, with the two set in Monsalvat flanking the central set in Klingsor's domain. The similarities between Acts One and Three are self-evident. Each begins with a forest scene, in which Gurnemanz and Kundry are later joined by Parsifal; both Acts are divided by a long passage of transformation music for the scene change to the Grail temple. In both, the choral ritual of the second scene is punctuated by a long solo passage for Amfortas. Yet there are parallels that extend across all three Acts, and that are no less obvious. In each Act there is a scene change, in each an extended choral passage. In each there is one solo or dialogue devised as a chief focus of musico-dramatic weight: Gurnemanz's

[1] *Debussy on Music* trans. R. Langham-Smith (New York, 1977), p. 167
[2] Cambridge Opera Handbook to *Parsifal*, L. Beckett (Cambridge, 1982), p. 84

narrative in Act One, the Kundry-Parsifal dialogue in Act Two, and in Act Three the exchanges between Gurnemanz and Parsifal which culminate in the Good Friday music. By saying that these three solo/dialogue passages are particularly important, we do not depreciate the two Grail scenes, awesome in every respect, or even suggest that the oddly static music of the Flower Maidens is negligible. But the choral scenes are, on the whole, more shut in upon themselves, musically self-sufficient. They are closely related to the orchestral preludes and interludes. This relationship is an abstract one; like the instrumental passages the choral scenes have a stronger character as purely musical edifices. In the case of the two Grail scenes there is also a specific relationship, for they are large-scale transformations of music from the Act One prelude.

The monologue/dialogue passages are, to the contrary, far more rhetorical. Here Wagner focuses on the poem, on the progress of the drama, and upon the creation of musical allegories that will comment upon these verbal phenomena. In creating these allegories Wagner has passed far beyond the innocent and lexical leitmotifs of *The Ring*, that fairy-story world where cetain themes are indeed literal musical signs for objects and characters. As in *Tristan*, most of the motifs in *Parsifal* have a less specific import; they refer only to extended families of images, and these only vaguely defined. Their multiple referential meanings tend to insinuate themselves into the listener's perception, rather than to hammer on his intellect.

For example, two well-known symbolic motifs in *Parsifal* — the 'Prophecy' and 'Magic' motifs [54] and [4] — are les simple-minded as musico-dramatic signs than mere labels might suggest. The 'Prophecy' motif is first heard in a weak, unfocused form [42], as one of the knights refers ironically to Gurnemanz's hope for Amfortas's recovery, 'You still can hope, you who all things know?' A few moments later, the motif has become more sharply delineated, when Gurnemanz refers obliquely to 'the one' who can bring salvation to Amfortas. When asked for a name, Gurnemanz turns his questioner aside; the motif is broken off in mid-phrase, and at the same time Kundry's sudden appearance points the orchestral fabric in another direction entirely. In these few bars, however, the 'Prophecy' motif [54] has been adumbrated and begins to coalesce, just as a first reference to 'all' that Gurnemanz knows — the accumulated histories he will later reveal — is narrowed down to a far more specific piece of knowledge, the still-untold story of the 'blameless fool'. The third time it appears, this thematic scrap is still richer, and has been expanded; now it accompanies Amfortas's broken quotation of the prophecy's actual words:

'Made wise through pity —' was it not   'Durch Mitleid wissend —' war's nicht
so?   so?

Just as Amfortas interrupts himself, so the motif's musical unfolding is broken off. The motif will not be spun into its syntactically complete form until the end of Gurnemanz's narrative, as he recounts in full Amfortas's 'holy vision'. Parsifal's precipitous entrance, hard upon the heels of Gurnemanz's cadential peroration, at last suggests a real identity for the 'blameless fool'. More than this, the similarity of Parsifal's entrance to Kundry's earlier entrance — both as if in answer to the riddle posed by the motif — is surely calculated as a comment on her status in the drama, for Amfortas's salvation will depend upon them both, upon their confrontation in Act Two, and not upon Parsifal alone.

The progressive realisation of the 'Prophecy' motif is both a musical and

Margarete Matzenauer as Kundry. A soprano who also sang mezzo roles, she was well-known for her Brünnhilde and Isolde and created the role of Kostelnička in the American première of 'Jenůfa' (photo: Metropolitan Opera Archives)

musico-dramatic process. A barely defined fragment gradually becomes a full musical phrase, and its recurrences are like tiny nodal points that articulate long stretches of the Act. At the same time, an unfocused reference to Gurnemanz's memories evolves into his memory of a single fact: the true words of the prophecy. The case of the 'Magic' motif [4] is far more complicated. The motif in its most familiar form is a chromatic variation of the pure, triadic 'salvation' motif [1a] from the Act One prelude. This sort of symbolic dualism was by no means new to *Parsifal*; it is ubiquitous in *The Ring*. But if we follow the musical evolution of [4], we find that its poetic associations are too rich to be subsumed under the single word, and seem as well to lie in another domain. The motif is prefigured as the merest fragment [43] when Kundry speaks the word 'Arabia':

GURNEMANZ

Tell me where it was found.	Woher brachtest du diess?

KUNDRY

From further off than your mind can reach:	Von weiter her als du denken kannst:
if this balsam fails,	hilft der Balsam nicht,
Arabia offers	Arabia birgt
naught else to soothe his pain.	dann nichts mehr zu seinem Heil.

Its next appearance, still as a fragment [43], is again tied to this single word, when Amfortas asks Gurnemanz where the 'strange mysterious flask' of balsam has come from. Within Gurnemanz's narrative, the motif [4] is extended to its fuller form for his description of Kundry's first appearance in the Grail kingdom, and his story of Amfortas's seduction:

Beside the walls	Schon nah' dem Schloss
virtue was snatched away...	wird uns der Held entrückt...
A fearful beauteous woman	Ein fürchtbar schönes Weib
holds him in sway.	hat ihn entzückt.

In this fuller form, the motif will also accompany Kundry's magic sleep, but it then disappears from Act One, not to recur until Act Two, at the moment the curtain parts to reveal Klingsor's necromantic laboratory. The motif's family of associations is thus a curious one; they congregate not only around the vague notion of 'magic', but around the idea of a place unknown, of terrain further away than Gurnemanz's 'mind can reach'. At first this is represented by Arabia, the country to the east, barbarian and occult. Near Klingsor's castle Amfortas is magically transported to a place inhabited by the 'fearful beauteous woman'; Kundry falls into a trance that will bring her from Monsalvat to Klingsor's castle. When the curtain parts in Act Two, that *locus* is at last revealed to the eye: this is the place that Gurnemanz's mind cannot reach, the darkest scene in the entire opera, the landscape from which the world's evil emanates. Wagner has, incidentally, so calculated the gradual evolution of the 'Magic' motif [4] that our realisation of its musical kinship with the 'salvation' motif [1a] (which dominates the end of Act One) should come with terrible irony as we first see Klingsor.

The musical and dramatic unfolding of Act One may be seen — albeit whimsically — as reflecting on a broad scale the kind of musico-dramatic realisation that we see on a small scale in these tiny motivic transformations. Gurnemanz's narrative is a realisation of the past. Histories, at first only known through allusions, will be revealed in stages that strike progressively deeper into their meaning. The initial action that leads up to the narrative is unusually swift for Wagner. Within a few moments Amfortas and his sickness

A scene from Hans Jürgen Syberberg's film of 'Parsifal' with Aage Haugland as Klingsor and Edith Clever as Kundry (Yvonne Minton sang the role) (photo:Artificial Eye)

have been mentioned, and Kundry has made her entrance. This opening is expository in character, for the chief thematic elements are introduced in a straightforward manner (for instance, Kundry's characteristic accompanimental figure [5]) and cut off almost brusquely, without lingering over their potential for development. In the scene of Amfortas's first appearance, Wagner begins to move towards a more structured kind of musical web: Amfortas's characteristic theme is reiterated through this scene as a refrain, though one both tentative and weak, prone to interruption by other musical elements. So far, then, Wagner sets up the plot and introduces the characters, and lays out a palette of musical elements that will be used in the course of the Act. This entire exposition prepares for the narrative, which will both clarify the histories presented by allusion, and develop musical material presented previously in bald and unelaborated forms.

Gurnemanz exposes the past but he will also — sometimes unwittingly — reveal both its secret meaning and his own reactions to it through his ordering of its events. Five stories are told: Kundry; Amfortas and the loss of the Spear; Titurel and the Grail; Klingsor; Amfortas's prophetic vision of his saviour.[3] The stories do not simply pass chronologically from furthest to most recent past; rather, they generate a temporal circle that will constantly and inevitably turn back to a single event. This event is Klingsor's wounding of Amfortas, a moment laden with mythic significance. The narrative is initiated when Gurnemanz defends Kundry against the taunts of the squires by describing her recent deeds helping the knights of the Grail ('when you are all perplexed'). This brief apologia is cast musically as a concise *Lied*; it begins and ends unequivocally in E minor, closed upon itself in a single key. So far Gurnemanz is a neutral narrator, certain of his story and detached from it. The passage's cool musical formality seems to admit no doubts. But Gurnemanz shifts from summarising Kundry's current exemplary behaviour to uneasier speculation about her past, and at the same time citations from symbolic motifs ripple the music's surface. For instance, the 'Prophecy' motif [54] in an unrealised version is called up to accompany the line ('Though she may serve us but as penance, yet the noble band of knights is grateful'). Again this rhetorical citation of the motif suggests Kundry's oblique part in Amfortas's salvation. As Gurnemanz sinks deeper and deeper into contemplation of Kundry, he recalls that she was absent once when a great disaster befell the knights; here he comes dangerously close to a memory of the Spear but evades it, and instead retreats further into Kundry's past history, and how Titurel found her long ago in the wood. Now, for the first time in the Act, the 'Magic' motif [4] is spun out, developing into a continuous accompaniment for Gurnemanz's words. This motivic motor builds in intensity as Gurnemanz himself becomes more agitated, and the Kundry narrative culminates in his angry demand:

Hey! You! Hear me and say: He! Du! Hör mich und sag':
where were you wandering on the day   Wo schweifelst damals du umher
when by our Lord the Spear was lost?   als unser Herr den Speer verlor?

In a brilliant stroke, Wagner sets the first three syllables of this text to a three note turn, Db-Eb-Db. This is a germinal musical cell from which the main motif for the next story will spring [1e]:the narrative of the Spear. Gurnemanz has now, at last, been led to his memory of it. The three-note turn

[3] Some commentators locate the beginning of Gurnemanz's narrative at the story of Titurel. This seems perverse, for it passes over the Spear narative, and ignores the musical link between all five stories.

48

and the motif which falls out of it so dominate this second history that all the musical substance of this narrative seems to be drawn progressively into its orbit. We even begin to hear the melodic turn at the apex of [4] as a variant of it; the turn is also used to set Gurnemanz's anguished cry, 'the Spear from his hand is sinking' [1e]. This briefest of stories is also the most concentrated in its motivic focus.

As if to defuse that intensity, Wagner interrupts the narrative with the entry of two squires from Amfortas's train. This brings time back to the present, while a corresponding reference to Amfortas's descending motif [45] recalls the last music we heard in that present, before Gurnemanz began his tales. But the interruption is in turn interrupted, when Gurnemanz in an aside mutters his last words in the Spear narrative, 'A wound it is that ne'er will close again.' The accompanying musical reminiscence [45] serves to eradicate the effect of Amfortas's interloping refrain, thus turning us back to the narrative mode, and to the past.

Though the squires have questioned Gurnemanz about Klingsor, he answers evasively with a story about Titurel and the Grail. This third story involves the first large-scale recapitulation in the Act, for Wagner here adapts and transforms the sonic fabric of the prelude, interleaving its serene, triadic material with the inexorable three-note turn of the Spear narrative, which resonates in an echo of its former musical force. Just as the 'Magic' motif [4] — the chief thematic element for the Kundry narrative — was embedded as a leitmotivic citation in the Spear narrative ('a fearful beauteous woman'), so the three-note turn [1c & d] developed symphonically in the Spear narrative is quoted symbolically in the Grail narrative, as Gurnemanz describes Christ's wound, 'which at the Cross received his blood'. Wagner has devised a pattern of musical links that serve one purpose in binding together the separate musical 'stories', but that also serve a subtextual, poetic purpose.

The Grail narrative ends with one of the strongest cadences so far heard in Act One, a triumphant orchestral crescendo spun from the Grail motif [25] to a full stop on an F# major triad. The last musical word appears, for the moment, to have been said. This entire narrative has, however, been an evasion, as Gurnemanz struggled to avoid his memory of Klingsor. It is a memory he cannot escape, and the luminous F# major triad collapses into a single low F# in the basses and brass. With this sound, Wagner sweeps away all previous musical substance; the recollection of the Act One prelude disintegrates. Above the single F#, Gurnemanz begins the Klingsor narrative, a musical arch whose outer sections are generated from [7], the motif specifically associated with Klingsor, a motif distantly related to the 'Magic' figure [4]. This arch is, however, unbalanced and awry. Its opening and middle sections are straightforward enough. Gurnemanz begins in good chronological order by describing Klingsor's more distant past, how he was attracted to the fellowship of the Grail, his sin of self-castration, and his subsequent exile from the fellowship. The description of Klingsor's flowering desert is set to deliberately contrasting musical material, an anticipation of the Flower Maidens' chorus in Act Two; this is the centre of the arch. A momentary return of [7] (at 'and many fell in foul disaster') would seem to signal a balancing return of the whole opening unit. But Gurnemanz's survey of time has once again circled back to its most perilous moment, to his memory of the Spear and Amfortas's wound. The imminent approach of that moment breaks the symmetry of the musical arch, and Gurnemanz must also break off: 'What happened you now understand: the Spear is held in

Warren Ellsworth as Parsifal and Donald McIntyre as Gurnemanz in the Good Friday meadow, Act Three, Welsh National Opera (photo: Clive Barda)

Klingsor's hand.' So the Klingsor narrative crumbles at its close to a swift succession of leitmotivic quotations, closed off by a last, faded repetition of [7].

The final story describes Amfortas's vision, and culminates in the statement of [54], the 'Prophecy' motif. Parsifal's serio-comic entrance interrupts and terminates the narrative, and subsequent dramatic events deal with other musical matters. The entire Amfortas narrative is in itself, however, part of a far-ranging process of anticipation and realisation. Like the Grail narrative, it derives much of its musical substance from the motifs of the Act One prelude. Where the Grail narrative transformed the prelude in recapitulating it, this narrative cites its music more closely. Most significantly, the Amfortas narrative returns momentarily to the Ab tonal colour of the prelude. In the choruses of the Grail scene the Act One prelude re-emerges both as a confirmed tonality (Ab) and as an 'edifice in sound', for the Grail scene, like the prelude, is endowed with a purely musical coherence which works on a very broad scale. The scene is drawn together by sustained thematic development, periodic rhythmic phrasing, deliberate formal symmetries and a relatively straightforward harmonic vocabulary. The forest scene is, as a whole, far more discursive; its musical units are conceived on a much smaller scale and are often simply juxtaposed with one another; its harmonic language is more ambiguous. Not surprisingly, the only profound musical interruption in the Grail scene is Titurel's eerie speech and Amfortas's long reply, an aria whose music looks back to the Spear narrative and to the transformation music, and which in turn foreshadows the musico-dramatic core of the second Act: the aftermath of Kundry's kiss.

Act Two opens with the only scene given over to Klingsor himself. His musical identity and his mythic status have both been established in Gurnemanz's narrative. That musical presence has both a fixed tonal colour (B minor) and a motivic component. Wagner's choice of B minor to represent Klingsor's realm was far from casual. The 18th and 19th centuries had endowed this key with a peculiar affect; for Beethoven it was the 'schwarze Tonart', the black tonality. Associations with magic, the supernatural and the malign were a strong part of its character. Within Wagner's works it would be used as an iconic key for the Dutchman and Hagen; it is also the tonal colour given to Alberich's curse. Indeed, it is possible to see Berg's 'Invention' on the pitch B♮ for the murder scene in *Wozzeck* as a last reverberation of this tradition, and a self-conscious act of homage to its earlier representatives. The key of B minor was evoked momentarily in Gurnemanz's Klingsor narrative, as a single node in a shifting, wandering harmonic design. Now in Klingsor's scene, B minor is given far greater weight as the tonic key for the entire passage, a stable centre to which all harmonic digressions will return. The symbolic key has taken on a true musical function as controlling gravitational force.

There are other ways in which the Klingsor scene is an extension of the Klingsor narrative. Both the narrative and the scene are musical arches whose framing outer sections are generated from repetitions and variations of [7], the 'Klingsor' motif. The narrative's musical arch was asymmetric, for its final section is summarised by a mere fragment of the 'Klingsor' motif [4]. The baroque shape of this narrative microcosm at first appears to be duplicated in the larger world of the scene. A seeming recapitulation of the initial orchestral web begins at Klingsor's 'fiery longings and scorching pain' but this recapitulation is quickly interrupted and abandoned, as if Klingsor cannot bear to confront his memory or sustain the musical mood. Yet this passage is only a false recapitulation; it is, significantly, not in B minor, and so has the motivic content of the opening without its symbolic tonality. Klingsor quickly recovers his self-possession, taunts Kundry, hears Parsifal's distant approach; his description of Parsifal's battle generates a passage of orchestral *Inszenierungsmusik* dramaturgically akin to that for Kurwenal's description of the ship in *Tristan* Act Three. Upon the dissolution of this scene-setting interlude, Klingsor is again left alone on stage. With a few bleak comments he re-establishes the verbal style of the scene's opening. At the same time, Wagner has shrunk the musical fabric into recitative, returning to the spare declamatory texture associated with Klingsor's initial words, 'The time is come'. The true recapitulation, the completion of the arch, comes only at Klingsor's last line, 'then I will be your master'. This orchestral recapitulation will be transformed into transition as the set changes to the magic garden, and a gesture of musical closure mutates into an introductory flourish for the new scene.

The Flower Maidens are in a perverse way musically analogous to the Grail knights. Both are choral groups whose music is tonally focused (hovering around Ab major) and rhythmically consistent, though the narcotic barcarolle rhythms of the Flower Maidens are wholly unlike the march figures of the knights. Of course, the Flower Maidens' musical presence is not literally related to that of the knights; rather, the two groups share these general musical characteristics. Their common tonal identity (Ab) obviously has no simple-minded symbolic import; it hardly means that Wagner wished to make some mysterious connection between the two groups. Yet the shared tonal focus does have a strictly musical consequence; it creates a vast tonal arch which spans the break between the Acts, and sets off by contrast the 'schwarze Tonart' of the Klingsor scene. Indeed, we can sense an even larger and vaguer structural palindrome lying behind this one. The Klingsor scene lies at its centre, the choruses flank the centre on either side, and at the outer reaches are Gurnemanz's narrative and the Kundry-Parsifal scene, both long and discursive, both revelations of the past. Such symmetries are not merely specious contrivances which we impose on Wagner's score. Wagner was, to be sure, no foolishly consistent structuralist. But his control of shape over long expanses of time was one of his great strengths as a dramatist. And surely when Kundry begins her 'Herzeleide' narrative we are meant to sense a tenuous link between the present situation and the last time we heard the telling of tales.

The Kundry-Parsifal scene is remarkable not for any real interaction between the characters but for Parsifal's metamorphosis. Although Kundry is hardly negligible in this process, she is strangely neutral. Her role is to impart knowledge, thereby enabling Parsifal to achieve a transformation she could not foresee, into a mythic hero she cannot control. The peculiar neutrality of her dramatic status has certain consequences for much of her music, which is often self-contained in a way that Parsifal's is not. That is to say, her music forges fewer links backwards or forwards to the remainder of the score. At least at first, she presents Parsifal with detached and self-sufficient musical statements, to which he must react.

But if some of her music is conventional, her entrance is most striking: she calls 'Parsifal' (the first statement of his name) to a falling 3-note figure [x] which becomes a critical thematic element elsewhere in the score, and which is derived from the 'Prophecy' motif [54x]. This figure outlines the triad of B

52

Bayreuth, 1882: Heinrich Winckelmann as Parsifal, surrounded by Flower Maidens (Royal Opera House Archives)

minor, set within a harmonic context that turns the sustained (and by now somewhat tedious) A♭ of the Flower Maidens to a wholly new tonal direction, towards G major, the key of the 'Herzeleide' narrative.

Kundry, like Gurnemanz, is a narrator but she uses story-telling in quite different ways. He explores and reacts to his own memories while imparting information to his listeners; she tells a story to elicit emotional responses from Parsifal, believing this will facilitate her seduction. Gurnemanz's narrative passes through many stories; each has a unique musical character and motivic presence, and within each there are frequent rhetorical outbursts and unconnected musical juxtapositions. Gurnemanz's idiom is rich and wonderfully unbalanced. Kundry's 'Herzeleide' narrative is almost banal in its formality. Monothematic, seldom departing from the rhythmic patterns established in its first bars, it is in effect a proper aria, based on [58], the 'Herzeleide' motif. It falls into clearly articulated blocks, beginning with two parallel verses ('I saw the child'; 'On tender mosses you were cradled') and a tonally contrasted strophe ('forever weeping'). This third verse in turn builds into sequential repetitions of [58] as Kundry descends into pathos ('So anxious was she, ah! and fearful'); this musical intensification and acceleration culminates with her rhetorical question 'Oh, did you not fear her kisses then?' The final section ('You were heedless') is a musical coda that varies [58] as part of an ostinato figure, and which concludes, rather primly, with a return of the opening [58], the original 'Herzeleide' theme, and the original key, G major. Wagner is playing here with the implications of

53

formality and coherence and, so long as Kundry is in control of the confrontation, she will retain this musical propriety. Thus the complete closure at the end of the narrative shuts it in upon itself; Kundry has made her first move with a perfectly fashioned musical statement.

Wagner's depiction of Parsifal's reaction begins with a critical musical symbol, as Parsifal cries, 'Sorrow, what did I?' His words indicate that he mourns his mother's death. But the vocal line [41] is Amfortas's, an almost literal quotation from the wounded knight's despair at Titurel's 'Must I die then without its light to guide me?' in Act One. This momentary musical association of Parsifal with Amfortas prefigures the entire dramatic course of the scene, for Kundry's kiss will set off Parsifal's transformation, his empathic identification with Amfortas. Here Kundry fails to comprehend the meaning of the musical sign. She continues to play on Parsifal's capacity for pity and sorrow, thereby creating a being she will find impossible to overcome. The musical gnomon is repeated a few bars later. Parsifal mutters obsessively, 'My mother, my mother, could I forget her?' and another fragment of Amfortas's aria materialises in the orchestra. This time, Parsifal literally seems to hear the musical symbol, for he suddenly asks, 'What else did I forget?' — just missing his own memory of Amfortas.

Kundry's reply ('Acknowledge your fault') is calculated — she believes — to convert Parsifal's new vulnerability into passion; both motivically and tonally she takes up a new musical argument, one conducted as a dialogue between the chromatic arpeggios of the 'Magic' motif and the precipitous descending flourish that is part of her own unique musical character [36]. At the moment of the kiss this musical dialogue ends with a long upward extension of the 'Magic' motif [4], whose final two notes (E#-F#) are slowly re-interpreted; they become the three-note turn (F-Gb-F) that spins into [1e], the 'wound' motif (F-Gb-F-Bb-C-Db). This is a metamorphosis that functions as a sonic analogue for the 'fearful change' that passes over Parsifal's features.

What follows is a passage that constitutes the opera's musical and dramatic heart [41, 36]. For Parsifal's revelation Wagner recalls the music of the climax of Amfortas's aria, his last despairing cry for mercy [34a & b].

It is an extraordinary moment. Parsifal literally becomes Amfortas, taking on the wounded king's musical identity as he does the terrible burden of Amfortas's suffering. This exact quotation from the aria is like the turning of a musical key that sets Parsifal's memory free. His subsequent monologue is both a recapitulation and a transformation of the aria. The basic sequence of musical events is the same in both monologue and aria but in Parsifal's hands the aria is converted into something musically richer and more exhaustive. Parsifal remembers what he once heard as a mere observer, and he lays over it a new palimpsest, a musical reinterpretation he can make because he is now *both* the observer *and* the one who is observed. Thus the 'recapitulation' of the aria's music is not just a far-reaching musical link between one act and another, but a brilliant musico-dramatic allegory. When Parsifal breaks his trance ('Thus rang his lamentation, fearful, loud, loud to my spirit. And I, a fool, a coward, to childish deeds of daring fled away!'), he loses his double vision, and the two musical entities — the remembered aria and the re-interpretation — become one, the remembered aria alone. For Parsifal's final words, 'Redeemer! Saviour! Lord of Grace! Can I my sinful crime efface?', Wagner simply adopts the aria's cadence, Amfortas's 'Take back my birthright, end my affliction.' Parsifal's visionary identification with Amfortas

54

anticipates their actual exchange of roles at the end of the opera, when Parsifal will take over Amfortas's office and receive his kingship.

All that follows Parsifal's vision must be faintly anticlimactic. Even Kundry's own conversion to supplicant, even the bleak, expressive recitative Wagner invents for her description of the Crucifixion, cannot approach the intensity, the layering of musical recollection, that characterises the visionary interlude. Indeed, once Parsifal returns from his vision to present time and place, we seem to return to a more operatic world, and frequent echoes of Tannhäuser and Venus are faint but unmistakeable. For the remainder of the scene Wagner devised a gradual musical *accelerando* typical of certain duet scenes in *The Ring* (notably the 'Annunciation of Death' in *Valkyrie*). The exchanges between the characters become briefer and briefer; there is a modulation of tempo from moderate to fast. Most importantly, the main thematic material from the earlier parts of the dialogue [58, 4, 34] will be stripped of its character and dissolved into a kind of frenetic orchestral wallpaper. Kundry's tale of her search for Christ ('I seek him now') is sung to an accelerated and rhythmically de-natured version of the slow chromatic line from [3x]; at the same time a rhythmic variant of that motif provides the orchestral background.

In the latter part of the scene, Kundry tends to convert a number of motifs into emphatic spondaic rhythms. This is not mere effect. As we shall see, Wagner is preparing, well within Act Two, one of the omnipresent sounds in Act Three — the grave, tolling rhythm that we hear from the first moments of its prelude [47].

As the acceleration in the scene reaches its peak, Wagner begins to make final gestures of closure by recalling music from the Act's beginnings. An accelerated version of the Flower Maidens' music [63] accompanies Kundry's ('so it was my kiss'), followed a few bars later by [57], the E♭ fanfare that had announced Parsifal's entrance, and finally [5], the 'curse' music from the Klingsor scene. These brief musical citations are patently purely musical flourishes, used in the service of a vague motivic summing-up at the Act's end; they do not occur as rhetorical responses to the poem. Nonetheless they do have a dramatic effect. With these three quotations, we are, so to speak, pushed backwards through the Act, from the Flower Maidens, through Parsifal's arrival, to the Klingsor scene. When Klingsor himself makes his final appearance, he has in a curious way been called up by this thematic retrogression; we have been led back to him. He will in this sense continue to resonate through the music of Act Two, even after Parsifal has vanquished him, for Act Two will end where it began: in the 'schwarze Tonart' of B minor.

We have seen Wagner's musico-dramatic arches operating on many levels but the largest of them is the arch formed by the entire opera, through the parallelism of Acts One and Three. Yet all the events shared by these two outer Acts take on new guises in Act Three; the world has been altered by Klingsor's defeat. The re-enactment of the Grail ritual now begins as a funeral march; Amfortas's prayer — punctuating this second Grail scene as his aria had punctuated the first — is a wish not for salvation but for death. Both individuals and landscapes have changed; Gurnemanz is 'grown very old', and Parsifal must ask, 'Do I err still? For everything seems altered.' Act Three is saturated by a sense of disorientation, of the disquiet that comes of being lost in a familiar place.

One way in which Wagner underlines the dramatic parallels between the

(Above) The Temple of the Holy Grail in Act One and (below) Parsifal heals the wound in Amfortas' side in Act Three of Götz Friedrich's production at Bayreuth, 1984 (photos: Festspielleitung Bayreuth)

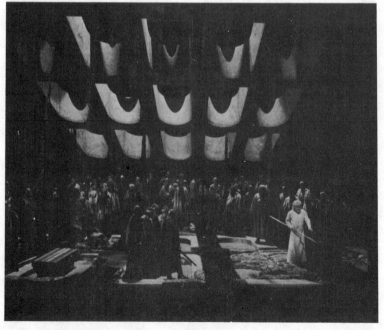

Acts is by engineering broadly conceived musical parallels. He underlines the profound changes in the opera's dramatic universe, however, with extensive alterations in Act Three's recollections of Act One. The mutation of Parsifal's motif for his Act Three entrance is only the clearest instance. The triadic fanfare [57], reminiscent of Siegfried, that announces his entry in Act One (and in Act Two), becomes muffled and uncertain in Act Three, ambiguous in its harmonic implications where before it was plain-spoken. The march for the Grail knights in Act One ('O Feast of Love undying') is straightforward in its melodic character and simple in its tonal language, beginning and ending in unclouded C major. The parallel funeral march in Act Three ('With sacred awe, concealed in this shrine') is dissonant, its melodic phrasing turned askew. This march glides perilously close to atonality, as does the nightmarish choral passage later sung by the knights as they press in upon Amfortas ('Reveal now the Grail!') [30, 43]. Thus in Act Three the apotheosis — Parsifal's healing of Amfortas, his ascent to the altar, the choral epilogue — comes as the greatest possible musical contrast, a recovery of the Act One prelude and its serene musical language in the face of nascent tonal dissolution.

Act Three is by far the most symphonic Act, in the sense that long stretches in it are either adaptations of the instrumental preludes or varied recapitulations of music from other Acts. The Good Friday music is, of course, literally symphonic. So compelling is its 'purely musical' logic that Wagner could detach it from the opera and deprive it of its words (if not of its dramatic associations) without making it nonsensical. Much could be written of the tremendous motivic and harmonic riches in any of these 'symphonic' passages; their musical meaning seems inexhaustible.

The 'symphonic' quality of Act Three befits the reflective nature of its drama, for Act Three is simply the dénouement, a long and slow-paced diffusion of tension. Everything that happens in it has been inevitable from the moment Parsifal won the Spear. It is an act of *tableaux* and rituals, such as the baptism or the Grail ritual; both involve extended borrowings from the Act One prelude. At such times, as during the Good Friday music, words themselves are treated as superfluous. These sustained musical edifices may be *au fond* symbolic in their 'purely musical' unities, associated as they are with points of stasis, meditation, ritual and resolution. Only in the brief pantomime for Gurnemanz and Kundry, and in the Parsifal-Gurnemanz exchanges, does Wagner compose for Act Three a musical idiom that reacts directly and consistently to the words it accompanies. Even here, as we shall see, the world has changed. The passage depicting Parsifal's arrival and his mimed gestures in response to Gurnemanz are one instance of Act Three's more rhetorical idiom. As Gurnemanz celebrates Kundry's recovery on the 'day of mercy past comparing', the triadic 'salvation' motif is extended into a brief six-bar orchestral passage, the first anticipation of the Good Friday music. The orchestral comment breaks off suddenly as Gurnemanz sees a figure approaching. For Parsifal's appearance, Wagner sets up a compound musical gesture that combines Parsifal's new, transformed 'fanfare', with a chromatic line ending on a falling figure B♭-E♮. This falling B♭-E♮ is a cell from the first bars of the Act Three prelude [47]. By referring to two notes from the prelude at this point, Wagner anticipates the fuller recollection of the prelude for Parsifal's first speech and Gurnemanz's reply to it. What is astounding about the figure here is that we do understand these isolated two notes as an echo of the prelude; Wagner has forced us to hear a motivic connection that resides in the tiniest of fragments. This falling B♭-E♮ is repeated over and over as Gurnemanz questions Parsifal and, for the moment, it serves as an inexorable cadential turn at which all music seems to end.

This motivic fragment is part of a musical dynamic which bridges the disparate, contrasting passages in the subsequent Parsifal-Gurnemanz dialogue (Parsifal's narrative of his quest and Gurnemanz's description of the recent history of the Grail). Both these speeches centre upon musical material from the Act Three prelude; Parsifal's is a development of the upward-rising figure derived from [5], Kundry's 'curse' motif. Gurnemanz's speech, however, takes up the rising and falling two-note cells of the prelude's first bars [1c, d]. Thus Gurnemanz makes a musical-mnemonic connection not only to the prelude itself, but to the enigmatic two-note cell that had clung so tenaciously to Parsifal's entrance. As his monologue reaches its peroration, the figure is broken down into accompaniment [49].

Here we begin to realise that a more far-reaching musical resonance is at work; this is the spondaic figure of Kundry's final, angry speeches in Act Two. At the same moment, Wagner gives a last turn to his motivic kaleidoscope. The spondaic figure passes into the bass to become the sound of four tolling bells from the Act One transformation music, at once a memory of the past, and a hint of what is to come. Wagner's final move in the game comes during the pantomime music, as Kundry runs to fetch water for Parsifal. The motivic flourish is given once again in the form associated with Kundry in Act Two [31], and then immediately as the music of the bells [30]. So Wagner summarises in a single instant the entire timespan of this series of transformations: from the conclusion of Act Two to the final scene of Act Three.

When we stop to consider it, we see that the process here at work is not unlike the dynamic of anticipation and realisation in Act One, the process that generated the 'Prophecy' motif [54]. But there is a critical difference, one that needs to be stressed as a concluding irony to our consideration of words and music in *Parsifal*. In Act One, as we saw, the gradual 'realisation' of the 'Prophecy' motif had a poetic meaning. The recurrences of the motif were called up by the poem; its transformation from nebulous to concrete reflected an analogous kinesis in the words it accompanied. The mutations in the motif were also musical commentaries on the language and on the drama. Here in Act Three, the motivic mutation just described is a solely musical phenomenon. The spondaic flourish has no meaning; it is not a sign; its recurrences are not determined by some poetic and dramatic need. In short, a specific procedure, used for dramatic and referential purposes in Act One, has become in Act Three a purely sonic event. Perhaps we can see in this a metaphor for the shift of balance from music-for-words to music-without-words as it extends through the entire opera. In the end, in the choral epilogue that closes the opera, *Parsifal* is indeed Debussy's 'beautiful edifice raised to the eternal glory of music'. Yet we should remember that just as Wagner did not always write disjointed, reactive music to symbolise words, so he did not always write merely 'pure' and unified music, in which the only drama needed is the abstract one of motifs, harmony and tonality. His real genius resided in his ability to modulate between the two, to be both pure musician and musical poet.

Discursions into the Dramaturgy of 'Parsifal'

Gerd Rienäcker

I. An anguished beginning: unison violins and cellos, supported by a clarinet and a bassoon, and then a cor anglais, intone a long-drawn-out melody — 'sehr ausdrucksvoll' ('very expressively') — grandiosely, in so far as the muted strings will allow. It is a veiled promise, already half-revoked.

The theme [1] rises from the depths, at first triadically and then stepwise, the minor second [1c] a surprise, suggesting further anguish; after six notes the ascent falls back upon itself, plunging downwards despite a new effort to ascend. It comes to final rest in a gently swaying figure. Yet here also there is a sense of retraction smoothing out the rise and fall, stilling the sense of movement.

The contours of rhythm and metre are blurred, the main pulses are awash and, gradually, all sense of time is lost. The extreme slowness makes it impossible to decipher the metre; the pace is vague. A sense of order, introduced by the dotted rhythm [1f] in the third bar, is quickly lost in uncertainty.

Orchestral colours remain undefined; almost imperceptibly the crescendo drives apart what had been fused before. The sound of the cor anglais at the climax fades away as the theme falls back, and leaves behind a sense of uncertainty.

The key of A♭ major can scarcely withstand this uncertainty; in the third bar, it collapses suddenly into C minor, where it stays — insecurely; when the movement stops, it is the mediant — C — and not the root note of the chord — A♭ — which has been reached; the brass chords resolve this uncertainty. If this major tonality is indecisive, its opposite implies what is definite: as the veil falls away, nothing less than the wounds of the Passion, emblems of death, are laid bare.

The melody binds them together in a psalmody reminiscent of chants of 'Kyrie', 'Gloria' and 'Alleluia' yet without form — a liturgy in the abstract. The ritual actions are evoked with mystic numbers: there are six notes in the ascent, seven notes before the collapse, and ten notes follow: five bars in all, centred upon the dotted note pattern in a summary of a divine ordering of the world, the act of creation, perfection in good and evil, the holy stigmata, the emblems of becoming, of the iron rule of the Grail, of unspeakable suffering.

An anguished beginning! Unforgettable because of its prominent position in the score, this motif breaks the stillness of the night-enshrouded space and enjoys an existence of its own before pointing ahead to what follows; for the message must be found in the music, and in what happens on stage — in the entirety and in the fabric of which it is made.

Act One, scene two; the knights of the Grail have assembled to receive Communion. Ecstatically, they listen to the sacramental words from the shadows — and to those words, drifting from above, the opening theme [1] is now given. It is often labelled the 'Love-Feast' theme.

Before this, it has been heard both in the rapt ecstasies of Amfortas and in the narrations of Gurnemanz; later, Parsifal himself will take it up. It circles frequently around the sacred chalice, around the wondrous forces which shelter within it, around spiritual salvation and redemption from sin; he who hears or intones its melody seems lost to the present, for his eyes remain fixed on the chalice in visionary contemplation, on a relic that may bring him grace and enlightenment: healing for those in need. The theme speaks of one who has fallen into adversity, of one or of a community gathered to receive Communion. (As a general rule, these themes do not just define stage properties but fundamental situations and character relationships; Wagner called them 'Grundthemen' not 'Leitmotiven'.)

The sound of torment within the vision is unmistakable; it suggests the agonised gesture of those in extreme suffering as they fall back when they try to raise themselves, and their anguished prayers. The sound is as unmistakable as the dotted rhythm of the ceremony of the petrified rule of the Grail, the rhythm which will later lead us into it. The psalmody itself evokes ritual, for it is only in ritual that the community of the knights of the Grail finds and preserves its cohesive strength, but also its sense of anguish.

Within the sacred chalice dwells the suffering Redeemer; it is of His body and His blood that the sacramental words tell; just as the words proclaim comfort for those in need through the experience of the Passion, so this music expresses the depth of their suffering; it is inextricably linked with those who seek and hope, with their search, and with salvation itself.

One of the crucial situations in *Parsifal* is thus expressed by these five bars which stand at the threshold of the work. The motifs which make up this theme provide a key to highly disparate events, actions and situations, and each develops into separate themes; the whole Prelude derives its ideas directly from this music. If the opening intervals of the triad are reduced from a third to a second and extended with five ascending notes, we have the motif associated with the Grail [25]. Stepwise intervals within the range of a fourth make up the motifs associated with faith [11], and with the Spear [1h]. The motif expressive of anguish [3] derives from [1h], with the addition of elements of [1]. Growing from the opening motif, the emergence of the motifs associated with the Grail, with faith and with suffering mark turning points in the drama, and each leads necessarily to the next.

The thematic spectrum broadens during the first Act without once breaking out of this web of musical derivation. Everything, literally everything, is related to the opening bars, whether it be the tired, sinking gesture of Amfortas [45], the four ascending notes of the Spear motif [1h], the oracular prophecy 'Made wise through pity, the blameless fool' [54] or the four-note chime of the Grail temple bells [30]. Furthermore, the strangely convulsive rising and falling motif which characterises Kundry — and later Klingsor — [7] together with the sharply falling motif with which Kundry and Amfortas [36] collapse to the ground, cannot deny their origins in [1]. The web of motifs spreads over the whole Act. It seems that even Klingsor and his magic realm are comprised in it.

What a deadly combination! Even in Act One, it provides a cryptic commentary on Gurnemanz's narration. Whenever there is a mention of the 'holy solemn night', of the sacred relic and the citadel Titurel erected around it, or his fierce campaigns against the infidel, of Klingsor's misguided search for salvation, of his revenge and his enchanted garden, we hear a wide variety of themes: the link between Klingsor's realm and that of the Grail is not apparent until we recognise that he fashioned it from the ruins of the Love Feast. It was the Grail which rejected him and turned him into its enemy. It is the Grail ceremonial and its petrified rule which hold the community together but make it at the same time defenceless against life and thus vulnerable to the enemy it has made for itself. In the last analysis, it was not

Dietrich Fischer-Dieskau as Amfortas at the Bayerische Staatsoper, Munich, in 1973 (photo: Anne Kirchbach)

Klingsor who inflicted the wound which afflicts Amfortas and, through him, the whole band of knights.

That Parsifal, the untouched, is increasingly drawn into the musical web of the Love Feast and that his own motif [57], not merely the prophecy motif, is fundamentally related to it is, on one level, the consequence of his entering the domain of the Grail. Thomas Mann has pointed out, however, that, through the 'associative magic' of Wagner's scores, there are parallels at a deeper level: while the sacred relic is hidden from the world, Parsifal was himself removed from the world by his mother Herzeleide, lest he should fall into sinful ways. In the eyes of the fugitive lad, the world contracts to a place of giants and robbers, whom he fights without knowing why; as he hurries from land to land, he is as far removed from the world as he was before. He encounters love in order to renounce it, since otherwise he would have been damned, or suffered the fate of Klingsor's captive knights. Stripped of his all-too-human frailties, he can belong to the Grail: for him, to cure those in need means to take their sufferings upon himself, sufferings which are bound up with the ritual and purpose of the Grail — but for ever?

'Redeemed the Redeemer': the epilogue to the *Bühnenweihfestspiel* is expressed in a transformed version of [1] or, more precisely, of the first half of the motif, which now ascends, without interruption, to radiant heights [2]. The falling interval has been expunged, the cry of lamentation has been exorcised.

And yet a curiously glass-like sound cuts short this 'redemption': has the breath of life itself been stifled when the wound was closed?

II. According to Wagner, the 'linguistic ability' of the orchestra lies in 'expressing the inexpressible'. The 'Grundthemen', which reveal more than words or stage events can convey, constitute, in Brecht's words, 'events behind the events' whenever they are heard. The actions, concepts, phrases or things which are associated with them are initials, rather than labels, but still convey a sub-text by articulating what no one is able or willing to say at the time. With increasing frequency, however, conscious silence passes into ignorance — the themes reveal that ignorance and function as external commentators on it; for instance, in his narrative Gurnemanz weaves an openwork texture of facts and silences for the squires; where he is silent about something it is not because he intends it for effect. He talks about the enemy but almost entirely fails to mention the one essential fact we need to know about Klingsor — his early history — and it remains unclear what he really knows about this; at the same time, the themes of Klingsor's rebellion and downfall permeate what he says, without his being conscious of it. Because this thematic web ensnares the characters whenever they try to convey important truths as messengers or teachers, it makes for a feeling of increasing entanglement; the drama responds to this sense of ensnarement more than the characters ever realise. It is not only Klingsor's motifs which surge through Gurnemanz's narratives; the motifs associated with the holy sanctuary envelop him also, loosening his tongue without enabling him to grasp the deeper meaning of what he says — he is merely permitted to lose himself in them. When, however, he consciously attempts to establish points of reference in order to know where he stands, to find a handhold to support himself on his way, he fails. He introduces Titurel, in his narrative to the squires, so that he can appeal to him directly, but the theme evaporates, for this bridge will not bear the weight to be placed upon it, and beneath it yawns an abyss. Nothing will prevent Gurnemanz from falling so long as he tries to construct such bridges for himself; if he allows himself to be led by events, however, they will yield the material he needs for understanding: it is not he who conjures up the organ-like music which descends, like some heavenly messenger, to help those in need; rather it is music itself which enfolds him and with its glad tidings snatches him from the edge of the abyss so that he may entrust himself to its celestial sound.

When instrumental passages — the 'Grundthemen' themselves and their development — express what the characters are prevented from saying or even knowing, they rob them of their roles as messengers. When Kundry calls Parsifal by name and, in doing so, appeals to the oracular prophecy of the blameless fool, she simultaneously betrays both knowledge and powerlessness: against her will she summons the action which the fool must now perform; as a result her mission will fail. At the same time the prophecy expresses the ineffable yearning to which she, for her part, dare not succumb — will the fool redeem her also? Nothing could be further from Parsifal's thoughts until a sudden shock causes him to sense the vacuum within him, and 'love's first kiss' recalls the wound of Amfortas. Waking dreams inspire him to act, cries of anguish drive him on; the Love Feast has become for him a nightmare from which he gradually divines his mission, a mission which he blindly follows.

'Events behind the events': in accordance with this perception, the real action has shifted into the orchestra. Above all, the preludes and interludes function as co-ordinating points, defining the basic dramatic situations even before words and actions have supervened.

Let us return to the beginning: the opening prelude contains three sections, of which the first introduces the motif of the Love Feast [1], the second the motifs of the Grail and of faith [25 & 11], and the last returns to the beginning. A triptych? It is as though an hermetic seal separates each of the themes and sections. Furthermore, whatever is developed is, or seems to be, revoked. Is this a denial of all-embracing connection, or of development itself? Although such a suggestion is inconsistent with the idea of thematic derivation, these derivations merely describe an arc which leads back to the opening theme; what concludes the entire prelude is projected by what concludes each section: a pause for repose and contemplation. Either way, there is no going back.

The 'liturgical' motif of the Love Feast does not reach the final section intact for its component parts grow increasingly independent. Its first notes are opposed, repeatedly, by its detached central section: three times the beginning is invoked but two or even three times the motif turns back on itself and falls away, so that the last ascending phrase is splintered. The cry of anguish, such as is uttered by those who suffer deeply, acquires a searing eloquence as it culminates in thrice-stated clouds of chromaticism. Yet even here the individual sections become detached and entangled in the motif of grief, before the climactic motif, descending interval and gently swaying figure again coalesce as a self-contained half of the theme: only at the third (!) attempt do they successfully fuse.

Thematic development, however concealed, assumes that the boundaries between the sections can be crossed without difficulty; bridging passages are incorporated into the texture, though they may not be immediately recognisable as such. These are governed by the art of the subtlest transition — adjacent chords combine unexpectedly to form the opening thirds of the Love Feast theme; a drum-roll leads into the last section, establishing and fixing its tonality — Ab — before this is undermined by the strings on F, a

Siegfried Jerusalem, one of the most recent exponents of the title role at Bayreuth (photo: Bildarchiv Bayreuther Festspiele)

third below. The structure, though solid, is permeable; what lies within is sealed off and introverted. There, where development seems impossible, it nonetheless takes place — surreptitiously. The circle is only half-closed. This concept imbues even the opening bars: the psalm-like melody returns not to the tonic key but to a third above; almost imperceptibly the motif broadens into a polyphonic web which absorbs the melody and elevates it. When this polyphony subsides, the motif has risen above it.

The 'liturgical' theme begins again on the mediant and abruptly changes its profile: the aspects associated with lamentation, barbed and contrasted, now emerge more sharply than ever, driving out the key of C minor (the climax of the motif — the dotted rhythms and the plunging interval — unexpectedly collapses onto the submediant, E minor). The sound is roughly burnished, increasingly fragmented, with oboes breaking any sense of continuity. That is not all: the first climax is followed by a second in the still centre of the swaying figure. At the same time, the motif returns full-circle to its starting point in this oscillating figure: the circle is no longer broken, and the jagged motifs float unresolved in space. The psalm-like theme has now sounded four times, and on each occasion it has led to something new, sealing it off or prising it open: it is as though, if the circle were to close, it would exclude something crucial. The final section in fact develops from what has been excluded and left unresolved. Here development and confusion exist together.

This is a mirror of the world of the Grail and, beyond that, of Kundry, Klingsor and Parsifal. Both their weaknesses and their strengths lie in their unbridled confusion. Their refusal to abandon responsibility for their actions keeps them alive, the very essence of their existence being to inflict innumerable wounds. The holy Love Feast reveals this. Although the ritual is couched in dark and ominously cold symbols, the music clothes it in garments of flame, which sustain it but give off no warmth. The opening motif of the prelude is built up gradually until it is transformed by a sudden ray of light: the music of violent grief, a cry of desperate frozen petrifying anguish. Titurel's supreme effort in his hymn of thanksgiving diverts the impending threat and stifles opposition. But the music only momentarily surrenders to him . . .

The Love Feast scene — and with it not only the sudden insight which causes Parsifal to tear himself from Kundry's embrace but even her vain search for her Saviour — is governed by the music of the opening prelude, and thus one of the fundamental situations of *Parsifal* is established. He who believes in it will find it difficult to have confidence in the innocent morning and undefiled Nature of the first Act. He will find it even harder to believe when he hears the distant motifs of the Love Feast and of grief, of the Passion and of salvation, while the squires are asleep. Furthermore, Gurnemanz's words imply the complications which the messengers from Amfortas describe, and which we ourselves witness in his suffering.

The end of the first scene is equally anguished. Gurnemanz and Parsifal set off for the temple of the Grail. A slow march has already supplied a framework for this: within this endless continuum time no longer exists. While the orchestra prevents the two men from speaking as they approach the temple, it now sets out to create a sense of time and development of its own. How unexpected are the motifs it summons up! First comes the tangled theme which Gurnemanz used to describe the defences of Monsalvat. With a sudden *forte*, dissonance builds to another climax with the chromatic motif of anguish. Because the cry of Amfortas is its centre, the march closes itself in a confusion of strangely languorous laments; there is a second outburst, with redoubled anguish, cut off by braying trombones: at the sound of the Love Feast motif, all else drops away.

The four-note tolling of the bells takes up the rhythm of the march; the *perpetuum mobile* creates the impression of walking on the spot beneath the temple dome. Although now silent, the music of the march anticipated the theme of the bells. It is logical that the orchestra should later pick up the motif again from the bells.

The interlude reveals all too clearly the link between the Grail ceremony and Amfortas' cry: it points to Amfortas, as the one to whom those in need turn for succour, and whom they will soon require to perform his holy office, although this will only perpetuate his pain.

The music conveys interminable oscillation between collapsing and rising. The four-note bell pattern seems to have shaped this figure . . .

Another marking would appear to govern the prelude to the second Act, 'violent, but not too fast' ('Heftig, doch nie übereilt'). There is a more sombre minor key and, from a chord sustained in the very depths of the orchestra, a semi-tone lower than the end of the previous Act, strangely distracted, wildly volatile motifs flare up; they are chained in the depths but restive, and plunge down again before they have reached the heights. The pattern of these movements — the rampant upward surge and the falling back — belongs to the main motif and overwhelms it to such an extent that, eventually, it will transform every phrase. Indeed, the sudden collapse here becomes the chief incident: this is the motif which characterised Kundry, Amfortas and even Parsifal when they fell to the ground in the first Act. Another familiar motif — the chromatically descending cry of pain — also emerges. Yet what has this to do with Klingsor's domain? It does not illustrate his magic tricks; instead it deftly characterises the basic situation from which this evil emanates. Its dramatic potential lies in its sudden rearing and plunging, in its sudden fits of uncontrolled energy; Klingsor is subject to its compulsive demands — countless times he rises to take the Grail by force, countless times he falls back into the dismal depths from which he wildly rises again, only to fall back once more — a thousand times he experiences rejection. As a result the idea of collapse becomes dominant, and the motif culminates in a piercing scream.

The motifs of anguish and collapse drive Klingsor and Kundry together, just as they drive Klingsor's enemies to him. All these motifs of wounding and falling exist in the prelude. The musical inferno lasts only fifty bars and its total disintegration anticipates the closing moments of the Act when Klingsor's tower collapses in ruins, Kundry falls to the ground and Parsifal, victorious but accursed, sets off into the wilderness with no idea where he is going.

To express this in music requires all the terrible armoury Wagner can muster: the tonal framework is torn apart — the music rushes wildly from one key to another, shrill dissonances combine with a piercing triad devoid of euphony; the colours fragment, and the motifs are harshly split; an abrupt change of register destroys every move towards melodic or harmonic consolidation; only a pale minor tonality, fanfares and a sense of restless wandering pull it together — at least until the ultimate point of utter disintegration when merely shard-like fragments remain. Each of these motifs permeates the second Act: the cry of anguish, the upward surge and downward fall, whether fleeting or protracted, the chromatic chord progression. Stripped of this restlessness, and linked to the themes of

66

Amfortas and the prophecy, these motifs are seen to derive from the motif of the Grail. For Klingsor seized all that he possesses from the Grail: his compulsive energy — his frenzied struggle to rise — is present in the prelude. So this introduction summarises what has gone before in order to build something terrifying from it; although this is Klingsor's music, it also mediates between both worlds. And is not this sense of feverish haste intimately related to the petrified ritual? Are they not the two sides of the same coin?

The answer to this question is given in the next prelude and the third Act: that Klingsor has been defeated by no means puts an end to his motifs, since they were associated with others besides him. The way through the wilderness, the desolation in the sanctuary, the deep distress experienced by Parsifal, the Grail knights and Gurnemanz, Amfortas' unspeakable anguish and the cry of blighted nature — all these motifs coalesce in an outpouring of grief which the prophecy motif in vain tries to oppose (as Klingsor and Kundry have previously been vanquished). The prelude does not allude to the fact that it is springtime; the natural cycle has no place in the wilderness in which mankind now dwells; it is not expressed until the Good Friday music. Then the music turns away from the blossoming landscape to devote itself to suffering humanity. Gurnemanz calls upon the music of the spring and Good Friday when Kundry returns, but to little effect. On Parsifal's return as a knight errant, he sinks once again to the ground, before rising as king and transcending his humanity; thus he seeks to come to terms with ritual and with nature.

Here also the fundamental situations are firmly established; the themes of the narratives of Parsifal and Gurnemanz, and even of the faltering knights of the Grail, return here; the Good Friday music annuls them only momentarily; whether Parsifal will definitively overcome them is an issue which can only be resolved in Utopia.

III. Wagner's *Bühnenweihfestspiel* is a summation of his life's work, a journey from opera to drama which incorporates the achievements and, indeed, whole passages from earlier works, most notably from *Lohengrin*, *Tristan and Isolde*, *The Mastersingers* and *The Ring*. The composer, a man of the theatre and would-be politician, has not rushed blindly into it. The origins of all that he has adopted are plain to see. Lohengrin's farewell to the swan is quoted when Parsifal kills the sacred swan and Gurnemanz bewails the hateful deed. Kundry approaches the blameless fool to the accompaniment of Tristanesque chromaticism and sustained chords; here the magic potion, by contrast, is, however, debased to necromantic skill. The Grail knights, in turn, have joined the Mastersingers' guild. And if the Grail theme is distorted to a grimace, it bears a fatal resemblance to Alberich's tarnhelm: it looks as though the squires in the first Act would like to deal with Kundry in much the same way as the Nibelungs sought to deal with the whole of the world.

There are many different reasons why Wagner reverts to traditional operatic forms. Recitative-like, arioso passages and even strophic settings are also a part of *The Ring*. If they emerge more clearly in *Parsifal*, it may be to give a clearer overall view of events. The striving for what Pierre Boulez has called 'legibility' is implicit in the orchestral writing, and it is in accordance with this principle that Wagner separates groups of voices and tonal layers, even where individual colours merge into one. Within a framework of tonal uncertainty, it is appropriate that the entry of 'Grundthemen' and their harmonic development should be clear. Operatic arias, recitatives, songs and ensemble passages each in their own way tell a story; to employ them begs the question as to the purpose of their original contexts, or, more pertinently, how Wagner interpreted their earlier use; from this emerge indispensable commentaries on the plot, and on the situations and characters.

Both Amfortas and Klingsor, in a *scena* and aria apiece, give eloquent and shattering expression to their suffering, but the traditional model literally breaks down beneath the weight. The accompanied recitative that leads into the aria, the introduction and the vocal entry apparently confirm our expectations: accompaniment patterns are clearly established before the main theme begins. Amfortas's *scena* is made up of an instrumental and a vocal four-bar phrase, almost identical to each other. But what happens within the four-bar phrase itself is strangely disparate; the theme fragments into two bars; wildly surging and plunging motifs in the cellos and basses scarcely affirm the accompaniment pattern but leap into the void; the chordal repetitions alter from bar to bar; within moments, however, the key of E minor is lost and Amfortas retrieves it from the minor third below, so that the fabric of his aria does not completely fall apart. While the opening is fragile and splintered, what follows is indecisive: admittedly, the exposition is followed by middle sections, but these cause the aria to sink into a series of orchestral images; only isolated, formalised motifs form a coda once the reprise has failed to materialise.

There could be no clearer picture than this of Amfortas's ensnarement: among images of collapse and ecstasy, of a desire conceived as guilt, of the sacred chalice and of failure, the *arioso* tradition breaks down: the series of images propels the singer forward; but disaster lurks even in the opening (apparently regular) two-bar phrase, in the familiar motifs of collapse and rebellion, which undermine the aria with their terrible interplay.

In the same way, Klingsor's aria announces its eventual disintegration: motifs that start up abruptly are cut off at the end of the bar and reduced to mutilated accompaniment patterns; two bars later, the main theme is introduced and distorted by Klingsor at his first entry; his haste, however, results from listening to the accompaniment pattern, the thematic grimace that develops from a previous act of violence. All the more obstinately does the music insist upon two- and four-bar phrases; where they assert themselves, all that they frame are scenes of devastation. In his attempt to escape this destruction, Klingsor desecrates the sanctuary, but it is precisely here that he fails: the final Grail chord turns into a shrill dissonance, and the cadence to which the music has been moving hangs in the air, preventing the aria from ending. Thus Klingsor's monologue projects on to the whole what its opening phrase had already described: the mutilation of his own limbs.

Nothing, it seems, could be further from such destructive motifs than the great ensemble scene known as the 'Waltz of the Flowers'. The four- and eight-bar phrases dance a charming measure, captivating the listener by their sheer regularity. Dainty arabesques entwine the dancers' limbs. A blessed isle?

Yet how strangely frail are these flowery garlands, for their elaborate periodic structure has begun in the meantime to fall apart: however unwavering the dance, groups of bars grow unhesitatingly independent, and not even the four-square structure remains intact.

The delicate strains of the Flower Maidens are shot through with fear, expressed in unexpectedly violent gestures: do they hint at danger? The

The Flower Maidens attempt to entice Parsifal (Siegfried Jerusalem) into their midst, Bayreuth, 1980 (photo: Festspielleitung Bayreuth)

flowers give voice to this thought: 'If you can't love us and woo us, we'll wither and languish away'. The fact that — as they tell Parsifal — their master plucked them in spring, not in autumn, reveals their tragedy: cut flowers court the favours of the blameless fool, his love-making must make good not only their lovers whom he has slain but also Nature herself from whom they have been torn — for a few moments only, before death intervenes.

The arabesques decorate that sinking gesture which we have identified as a cry of anguish. And the gently rising melody has about it aspects of the Love Feast theme, or at least of a mutilated version of it. Throughout the dance we sense the 'welling of sinful blood', a concealed motif which rears up rebelliously and then fades away.

Although redolent of transience, powerlessness and inchoate fear, the dance scene observes the devious rules of a game: for, like a succession of knights before him, Parsifal is to be drawn into Klingsor's realm: while the fallen flowers dance around him, Kundry waits ready to hand him over — against her will — to Klingsor.

An ensemble scene that seeks to confuse the senses is subject to censure: in *Art and Revolution* Wagner called opera 'a chaos that confuses the senses', the shrine of a mercantile god and the organon of industrialised amusement. That he developed the rules of opera to excess, causing them to crumble away gradually and imbuing them with symbols of death and the sounds of a veiled lament, throws a harsh light on Klingsor's domain and those who might fall under its sway. One cannot fail to hear the references to the Grail motif here, to the king's lament and to the ritual words of the Love Feast. More than that: Klingsor's evil presence lurks behind the flowers' seduction song; plucked and

69

fallen, the flowers, too, beg for love and tacitly hope for redemption.

It is opera itself that stands in need of redemption, that same culture industry for which Klingsor's deceitful ways are at least in part to blame: once its want of freedom has been subsumed, Nature herself may come into her own. The sage of Bayreuth allows an old vision of the future to speak anew: his festival later bore those musical visions to their grave. Only for a moment does a single self-contained musical structure belong to Nature — the Good Friday music; for here, and only here, does the Grail theme take on a lyrical aspect, a natural adaptable growth which in that way may learn to sing without restraint. A funeral march soon leads back within walls of stone to the world of ritual; amid such suffering, it also expresses Parsifal's farewell to his childhood and to his newly-awakened love; once more it leads into the thunderous peal of the bells; within the temple dome the knights of the Grail, crushed and broken, perform their melancholy rite, inflexible and leaderless, remote from Nature which alone can redeem them. When Parsifal returns the sacred Spear, he encounters a 'glass-bead game' which stylises the ritualised want of freedom by raising it without annulling it into celestial harmonies.

Even the work's description as a 'Stage Dedication Festival Play' is pregnant with ritual. It evokes tradition: the old Roman liturgy, polyphonic sacred music, a 'Dresden Amen' from the eighteenth century and, finally, Bach's *St Matthew Passion* — an immense force behind the *Bühnenweihfestspiel* from which the Bayreuth master has borrowed — in outline — a number of phrases sung by Christ, most notably his prayers on the Mount of Olives, together with the opening of the chorale 'Wenn ich einmal soll scheiden' ('Be near me, Lord, when dying'), closing suspended dissonances, and even the astringent sounds of the oboe.

Such borrowings tell their own story: as Amfortas and, later, Parsifal suffer the Saviour's wounds and experience his cry they take over His pain; the musical language of Bach comes to their aid.

Palestrina's style pervades the celestial choruses, turning them into abstract messengers of salvation, the incarnation of divine ecstasy. The muted woodwind which underpin the bells may conjure up organ sound.

This archaising trend itself becomes eloquent: a backward glance may give strength to those who are lost, while revealing the Passion to them. Everywhere there are signs of irresolution: polyphony leads to stark dissonances; a strangely intransigent note drives away consonance; not only chromatic but especially diatonic progression destroys the harmonic context, since chords permanently cloud over, layers of chords and orchestral voices overlap, and the result is bitonality.

In this there is a message for Wagner's successors: Mahler would adopt it, as would Debussy, Schoenberg and even Stravinsky, whatever the latter's objections to *Parsifal* may have been. Not only in music is new ground broken — a process strikingly akin to archaisation —, dramaturgically, too, there is much that is new. The montage and development of 'Grundthemen' might play right into the hands of the cinema; the use of intervention in the form of a radical commentary, combined with the dialectic of formal and stylistic criticism, might find a home in epic theatre, without finding a pigeon-hole for Wagner as a precursor of Brecht, Piscator or Mayerhold.

At the same time Wagner's return to the past is transformed into its antithesis: as he departs, he throws open doors; what he develops in his later works remains unrequited. That is, if one knows how to read these works properly, with one's eyes fixed ahead.

Thematic Guide

devised by
Lionel Friend

72

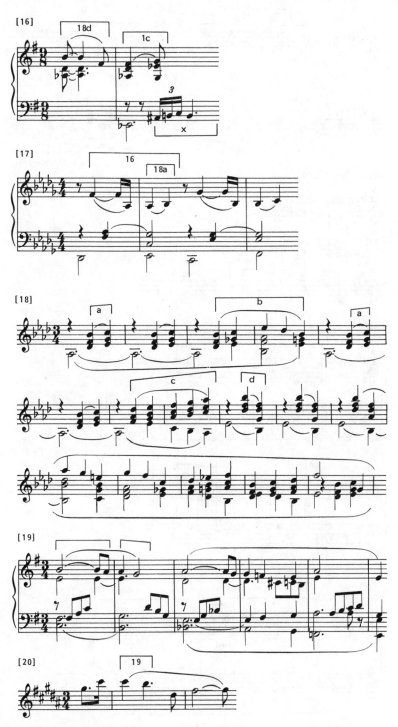

73

borrowed
from "Lohengrin"

also

74

75

[53]

[54]

(through pi – ty knowing, the blame – less fool:
"durch Mit – leid wissend, der rei – ne Tor,

x

42 42

wait for him, the one I choose)
har – re sein, den ich er – kor."

[55]

54

[56]

6 6 6

[57]

3

79

[60]
Who is good?
Wer ist gut?

[61]
(A - rise!)
Her- auf!

Yvonne Minton as Kundry and Peter Hoffmann as Parsifal in the 1979 production at Covent Garden by Terry Hands, designed by Farrah (photo: Reg Wilson)

Parsifal

Stage Dedication Festival Play
in Three Acts by Richard Wagner

Poem by Richard Wagner

English translation by Andrew Porter

Parsifal was first performed at the Festspielhaus, Bayreuth on July 26, 1882. The first performance in the United States was at the Metropolitan Opera House, New York on December 24, 1903. The first performance in England was at Covent Garden on February 2, 1914.

The stage directions are literal translations of those written by Wagner and do not reflect any actual production. The numbers in square brackets refer to the Thematic Guide.

The translation was made for,
and with admiration, affection and gratitude
is dedicated to, Sir Reginald Goodall.

Andrew Porter

Amfortas *son of Titurel and ruler of the*   bass-baritone
Kingdom of the Grail
Titurel *former ruler*   bass
Gurnemanz *a veteran Knight of the Grail*   bass
Klingsor *a magician*   bass
Parsifal   tenor
Kundry   soprano
First and Second Knights   tenor and bass
Four Squires   sopranos and tenors
Six of Klingsor's Flower Maidens   sopranos

Brotherhood of the Knights of the Grail, Youths and Boys, Flower
Maidens

*The scene is laid first in the domain and in the castle of the Grail's
guardians, Monsalvat, where the country resembles the northern
mountains of Gothic Spain; afterwards in Klingsor's magic castle on the
southern slope of the same mountains which looks towards Moorish
Spain. The costume of the Knights and Squires resembles that of the
Templars: a white tunic and mantle; instead of the red cross, however,
there is a dove flying upwards on scutcheon and mantle.*

*The Temple of the Holy Grail in Act One of Wieland Wagner's production at Bayreuth in
1968 (photo: Festspielleitung Bayreuth)*

Act One

A forest, shadowy and impressive, but not gloomy. Rock-strewn ground. A clearing in the middle. Left rises the way to the castle of the Grail. The background slopes steeply down in the centre to a forest lake. Daybreak. Gurnemanz (elderly but still vigorous) and two youthful squires are lying asleep under a tree. From the left, as if from the castle, sounds a solemn reveille on trombones. [1a]

GURNEMANZ
(*waking and rousing the squires*)

He! Ho! Wood guardians you?　　　　　He! Ho! Waldhüter ihr,
Sleep guardians I call you:　　　　　Schlafhüter mitsammen,
awake at least with the morning.　　　so wacht doch mindest am Morgen.

The two squires leap up. [25]

Hear you the call? Give thanks to God　　Hört ihr den Ruf? Nun danket Gott,
that He has chosen you to hear it!　　　dass ihr berufen ihn zu hören!

He sinks to his knees with the squires and joins them in silent morning prayer [11, 25]: *as the trombones cease, they slowly rise.*

Now up, young pages! See to the bath;　[12,53]Jetzt auf, ihr Knaben! Seht nach dem Bad.
time now for you to greet our master.　[45]　Zeit ist's des Königs dort zu harren.
The sickbed of the King is near,　　　[51]　Dem Siechbett das ihn trägt, voraus
I see the heralds on their way!　　　　　seh ich die Boten schon uns nahn!

Two knights enter.

Hail there! How fares our King today?　[45]　Heil euch! Wie geht's Amfortas heut?
He comes far earlier than usual:　　　　Wohl früh verlangt er nach dem Bade:
the balsam that Gawain　　　　　　　das Heilkraut, das Gawan
with skill and daring boldly won,　　　mit List und Kühnheit ihm gewann,
I'm hopeful that it eased his pain.　　　ich wähne, dass es Lindrung schuf?

SECOND KNIGHT

You still can hope, you who all things　[42]　Das wähnest du, der doch alles weiss?
　　know?
His pain returned more keenly,　　　　Ihm kehrten sehrender nur
　　more grievous than before:　　　　die Schmerzen bald zurück:
sleepless and racked with anguish,　　schlaflos von starkem Bresten,
he bade us swift prepare the bath.　　befahl er eifrig uns das Bad.

GURNEMANZ
(*sadly bowing his head*)

Fools we are, to seek for balm to ease him:　[54]　Toren wir, auf Lindrung da zu hoffen,
one single healing cures him!　　　　wo einzig Heilung lindert!
We search for balsams, soothing potions,　　Nach allen Kräutern, allen Tränken
search in vain far through the world:　[42]　forscht und jagt weit durch die Welt:
　　there is but one thing,　　　　　　ihm hilft nur eines,
　　　　only one man!　　　　　[54]　　nur der Eine!

SECOND KNIGHT

Tell us his name!　　　　　　　　So nenn uns den!

GURNEMANZ
(*evasively*)

　　See to the bath!　　　　　　　Sorgt für das Bad!

The two squires, who have returned to the background, look off right.

SECOND SQUIRE

But look, who's wildly riding here!　　Seht dort, die wilde Reiterin!

FIRST SQUIRE

Hey! The mane of the devil's mare is　　Hei! Wie fliegen der Teufelsmähre die
　　streaming!　　　　　　　　　Mähnen!

SECOND SQUIRE

Ha! Kundry's here!	Ha! Kundry dort?

FIRST SQUIRE

She brings some weighty tidings?	Die bringt wohl wicht'ge Kunde?

SECOND SQUIRE

Her mare is stumbling.	[5] Die Mähre taumelt.

FIRST SQUIRE

Flew she through the air?	Flog sie durch die Luft?

SECOND SQUIRE

She's falling upon the ground.	Jetzt kriecht sie am Boden hin.

FIRST SQUIRE

With her mane she's wiping the grass.	Mit den Mähnen fegt sie das Moos.

They all eagerly look off right. [23]

SECOND KNIGHT

The rider has flung herself off.	Da schwingt sich die Wilde herab.

Kundry rushes in, almost staggering. She is in wild garb, her skirts tucked up by a snakeskin girdle with long hanging cords, her black hair loose and dishevelled, her complexion deep ruddy-brown, her eyes dark and piercing, sometimes flashing wildly, more often strangely fixed and staring. [36] *She hurries to Gurnemanz and presses on him a small crystal phial.* [52]

KUNDRY

Here! Take it! Balsam . . .	Hier! Nimm du! Balsam . . .

GURNEMANZ

Tell me where it was found.	Woher brachtest du dies?

KUNDRY

From further off than your mind can reach:	Von weiter her als du denken kannst:
if this balsam fails, [43]	hilft der Balsam nicht,
Arabia offers	Arabia birgt
naught else to soothe his pain.	dann nichts mehr zu seinem Heil.
Ask no further!	Fragt nicht weiter!

She throws herself on the ground.

I am weary.	Ich bin müde.

A procession of squires and knights appears from the left, carrying and escorting the litter on which lies Amfortas. [45] *Gurnemanz has at once turned from Kundry to the approaching company.*

GURNEMANZ
(*as the procession reaches the stage*)

He nears; they bear him on the litter.	Er naht, sie bringen ihn getragen.
Ah woe! Can I thus bear to see him,	Oh weh! Wie trag ich's im Gemüte,
when in the pride of flowering manhood,	in seiner Mannheit stolzer Blüte,
the proud king of a conquering race [13]	des siegreichsten Geschlechtes Herrn,
is to his sickness made a slave! [1f]	als seines Siechtums Knecht zu sehn!

(*to the squires*)

Be careful! Hear, our master groans. [10,11]	Behutsam! Hört, der König stöhnt.

The squires halt and set down the litter.

AMFORTAS
(*raising himself a little*)

Good so! My thanks. A moment's rest!	Recht so! Habt Dank! Ein wenig Rast.
An anguished painful night [45]	Nach wilder Schmerzensnacht
now yields to morning's light. [51, 40]	nun Waldes Morgenpracht!

86

The holy lake	Im heil'gen See
will make my sufferings lighter:	wohl labt mich auch die Welle:
it soothes my woe; [45]	es staunt das Weh,
my night of pain grows brighter. [1h]	die Schmerzensnacht wird helle.
Gawain!	Gawan!

SECOND KNIGHT

Sire! Gawain is not here;	Herr! Gawan weilte nicht;
for when the healing herb	da seines Heilkrauts Kraft,
he strove so hard to bring you	wie schwer er's auch errungen,
proved to be of no avail,	doch deine Hoffnung trog,
upon another search at once he ventured.	hat er auf neue Sucht sich fortge-
	schwungen.

AMFORTAS

Unbidden? May he not regret it,	Ohn Urlaub! Möge das er sühnen,
to leave before the Grail commands! [25]	dass schlecht er Gralsgebote hält!
Oh, woe to him, so boldly daring,	Oh wehe ihm, dem trotzig Kühnen,
if he in Klingsor's snares should fall!	wenn er in Klingsors Schlingen fällt!
And so let none presume to help me!	So breche keiner mir den Frieden!
I wait for one, the one appointed:	Ich harre des, der mir beschieden
"Made wise through pity," [54]	"durch Mitleid wissend"
was it not so?	war's nicht so?

GURNEMANZ

You told us it was so.	Uns sagtest du es so.

AMFORTAS

"The blameless fool."	"Der reine Tor."
I think that I can name him: [9]	Mich dünkt, ihn zu erkennen:
for soon as Death I'll claim him.	dürft ich den Tod ihn nennen!

GURNEMANZ
(handing Kundry's phial to Amfortas)

First, my lord, please see if this will help [52]	Doch zuvor versuch es noch mit diesem!
you.	

AMFORTAS
(examining it)

Whence came this strange, mysterious	Woher dies heimliche Gefäss?
flask?	

GURNEMANZ

For you from far Arabia it was brought. [43]	Dir ward es aus Arabia hergeführt.

AMFORTAS

And who has brought it?	Und wer gewann es?

GURNEMANZ

There lies the wild maid. [5, 36]	Dort liegt's — das wilde Weib.
Up, Kundry! Come!	Auf Kundry! Komm!

Kundry refuses and remains on the ground.

AMFORTAS

You, Kundry? [36]	Du Kundry?
Again I have to thank you, [39]	Muss ich dir nochmals danken,
you shy and restless maid?	du rastlos scheue Magd?
'Tis well, your balsam now I mean to try:	Wohlan, den Balsam nun versuch ich noch:
I give you thanks for your devotion.	es sei aus Dank für deine Treue.

KUNDRY
(writhing uneasily on the ground) [36]

Not thanks! Ha, ha! How can it help you?	Nicht Dank! Ha, ha! Was wird es helfen?
Not thanks! Be off — your bath!	Nicht Dank! Fort, fort — ins Bad!

Amfortas gives the signal to move on. The procession passes into the far background. Gurnemanz, gazing sadly after it, and Kundry, still stretched on the ground, remain. Squires come and go. [45, 40]

THIRD SQUIRE
(*a young man*)

Hey, you, there! Still lying there
like a savage beast?

He, du da! Was liegst du dort
wie ein wildes Tier?

KUNDRY

Are the creatures here not holy? [25] Sind die Tiere hier nicht heilig?

THIRD SQUIRE

Yes! But if you are holy, [40] Ja! doch ob heilig du,
of that we are not so sure. das wissen wir grad noch nicht.

FOURTH SQUIRE
(*likewise a young man*)

And with her magic balm, maybe [5] Mit ihrem Zaubersaft, wähn ich,
she'll harm our master, even destroy him. [36] wird sie den Meister vollends verderben.

GURNEMANZ

Hm! Has she done harm to you?
When you are all perplexed,
and wonder how you can get news
to distant brothers fighting afar off
and hardly know where to send,
she, while you are still in debate, [5]
comes and goes on wings of the wind,
to bear your tidings and bring reply.

Hm! Schuf sie euch Schaden je?
Wann alles ratlos steht,
wie kämpfenden Brüdern in fernste Länder
Kunde sei zu entsenden
und kaum ihr nur wisst, wohin?
Wer, ehe ihr euch nur besinnt,
stürmt und fliegt dahin und zurück,
der Botschaft pflegend mit Treu und
Glück?

You feed her not, you house her not,
she has nothing in common with you:
but when you're in need
she gives her aid,
with zeal she flies to do your will,
and never asks one word of thanks.
I ask you, is this harmful,
when nothing but good she brings you?

Ihr nährt sie nicht, sie naht euch nie,
nichts hat sie mit euch gemein:
doch wann's in Gefahr
der Hilfe gilt,
der Eifer führt sie schier durch die Luft,
die nie euch dann zum Danke ruft.
Ich wähne, ist dies Schaden,
so tät er euch gut geraten.

THIRD SQUIRE

She hates us though; [40] Doch hasst sie uns;
just look, see how her eyes are flashing sieh nur wie hämisch dort nach uns sie
hate! blickt!

FOURTH SQUIRE

She's a heathen maid, [5] Eine Heidin ist's,
a sorceress. [36] ein Zauberweib.

GURNEMANZ

Yes, under a curse she well may lie. [42] Ja, eine Verwünschte mag sie sein.
Now she lives here, [60] Hier lebt sie heut,
perhaps renewed, vielleicht erneut,
to atone for guilt she may be driven, [1a,36] zu büssen Schuld aus früherem Leben,
some former guilt still unforgiven. [1h] die dorten ihr noch nicht vergeben.
Though she may serve us but as a [1a,54] Übt sie nun Buss in solchen Taten,
penance,
yet the noble band of knights is grateful: die uns Ritterschaft zum Heil geraten,
good are her deeds, [11] gut tut sie dann
from them we can tell: und recht sicherlich,
she helps us ... [39] dienet uns
herself as well. und hilft auch sich.

88

And so, perhaps, that guilt of hers [43] So ist's wohl auch jen' ihre Schuld,
brought upon us our great distress? die uns so manche Not gebracht?

GURNEMANZ
(*recollecting*)

True, when so long she stayed away from Ja, wann oft lange sie uns ferne blieb,
us,
then cruel misfortune came to pass. dann brach ein Unglück wohl herein.
I long have known her well: Und lang schon kenn ich sie:
but Titurel knew her still longer. doch Titurel kennt sie noch länger.

(*to the squires*)

He found her, when first he built our [4] Der fand, als er die Burg dort baute,
castle,
asleep among the bushes here, sie schlafend hier im Waldgestrüpp,
benumbed, lifeless, as dead. erstarrt, leblos, wie tot.
Thus I myself did find her lately, So fand ich selbst sie letzlich wieder
when our misfortune came to pass, als uns das Unheil kaum geschehn,
when that foul schemer over the das jener Böse über den Bergen
mountains
so shamefully assaulted us. so schmählich über uns gebracht.

(*to Kundry*)

Hey! You! Hear me and say: [25,36] He! Du! Hör mich und sag:
Where were you wandering on the day wo schweiftest damals du umher,
when by our lord the Spear was lost? [43] als unser Herr den Speer verlor?
Kundry is gloomily silent.
On that day why did you not help? [4] Warum halfst du nur damals nicht?

KUNDRY

I give no help. Ich helfe nie.

FOURTH SQUIRE

She says it herself. Sie sagt's da selbst.

THIRD SQUIRE

If she's so true, and free of fear, Ist sie so treu, so kühn in Wehr,
then send her off to fetch our missing so sende sie nach dem verlornen Speer!
Spear!

GURNEMANZ
(*gloomily*)

That's for another ... [1e] Das ist ein andres,
That task we're denied. jedem ist's verwehrt.

(*with deep emotion*)

O wounding, wonderful, all-holiest Spear! [1h] O wunden wundervoller heiliger Speer!
I saw you wielded by unholiest hand! [42] Ich sah dich schwingen von unheiligster
Hand!

(*absorbed in recollection*)

Thus surely armed, Amfortas, [1e, 1h] Mit ihm bewehrt, Amfortas,
boldly daring, Allzukühner,
what power could prevent you wer mochte dir es wehren,
from vanquishing the enchanter? [13] den Zauberer zu beheeren?
Beside the walls [53] Schon nah dem Schloss
virtue was snatched away ... [4] wird uns der Held entrückt:
a fearful beauteous woman ein fürchtbar schönes Weib
holds him in sway, hat ihn entzückt;
her warm embraces he is drinking, in seinen Armen liegt er trunken,
the Spear from his hand is sinking. [9, 1e, 1h] der Speer ist ihm entsunken.
A deathly cry! [36] Ein Todesschrei!
To him I fly! Ich stürm herbei:
See mocking Klingsor standing there, [4] von dannen Klingsor lachend schwand,
with impious hand grasping the spear. [1i] den heilgen Speer hatt' er entwandt.
The King escaped Des Königs Flucht
I guarded his returning; [9] gab kämpfend ich Geleite;
but he was wounded, [1e] doch eine Wunde

in his side the wound was burning:		brannt ihm in der Seite:
a wound it is	[1i]	die Wunde ist's,
that ne'er will close again.		die nie sich schliessen will.

The first and second squires return from the lake. [45]

THIRD SQUIRE
(*to Gurnemanz*)

So then you knew Klingsor?	So kanntest du Klingsor?

GURNEMANZ
(*to the two returning squires*)

How fares	Wie geht's
our King now?	dem König?

FIRST SQUIRE

He seems refreshed.	[40]	Ihn frischt das Bad.

SECOND SQUIRE

The balsam eased his pain.	Dem Balsam wich das Weh.

GURNEMANZ
(*to himself*)

A wound it is that ne'er will close again!	[45]	Die Wunde ist's, die nie sich schliessen will!

The third and fourth squires have already sat down at Gurnemanz's feet; the other two join them under the great tree.

THIRD SQUIRE

But Gurnemanz, say: we long to know:	Doch Väterchen, sag und lehr uns fein:
you once knew Klingsor — how was that[45, 60] du kanntest Klingsor, wie mag das sein?	
so?	

GURNEMANZ

Titurel, our noble lord, he knew him well.	[12]	Titurel, der fromme Held, der kannt ihn wohl.
To him, when evil forces showed their might,		Denn ihm, da wilder Feinde List und Macht
and he the realm of faith defended,		des reinen Glaubens Reich bedrohten,
To him there came one holy solemn night	[14]	ihm neigten sich in heilig ernster Nacht
our blessed Saviour's angels descending:	[25]	dereinst des Heilands selige Boten:
they brought the Cup used at the Last Supper,	[1]	daraus er trank beim letzten Liebesmahle,
the blessed Cup, that glorious holy relic,	[25]	das Weihgefäss, die heilig edle Schale,
which at the Cross received His sacred blood:	[8, 1f]	darein am Kreuz sein göttlich Blut auch floss,
they brought the Spear as well, which shed that flood.	[1h]	dazu den Lanzenspeer, der dies vergoss,
These tokens of God's love, of wondrous worth,	[14]	der Zeugengüter höchstes Wundergut,
to Titurel they gave to guard on earth.		das gaben sie in unsres Königs Hut.
For them he built our mighty sanctuary.	[25]	Dem Heiltum baute er das Heiligtum.
And to its service you were bidden		Die seinem Dienst ihr zugesindet
by pathways from all sinners hidden;		auf Pfaden, die kein Sünder findet,
you know that here no other		ihr wisst, dass nur dem Reinen
save pure in heart, as brother		vergönnt ist sich zu einen
may enter; to those who work the will of Heaven		den Brüdern, die zu höchsten Rettungswerken,
the Grail's most wondrous might is given.		des Grales Wunderkräfte stärken.
So, it was to him, of whom you ask, denied,		Drum blieb es dem, nach dem ihr fragt, verwehrt,
Klingsor, though eagerly and long he tried.		Klingsorn, wie hart ihn Müh auch d'rob beschwert.
Yonder the valley where he made his dwelling;	[7]	Jenseits im Tale war er eingesiedelt;
beyond it lie luxuriant heathen lands.		darüberhin liegt üpp'ges Heidenland:

I knew not what sin he there committed; [4]
he sought atonement for it, yes, holy he
  would be!
Unable to kill the sinful, raging lust within
  him,
his hand upon himself he turned
to gain the Grail for which he yearned,
and by its guardian he with scorn was
  spurned.
Afire with rage, then Klingsor swiftly
  learned,
how his unholy, shameful deed
to evil, unholy craft could lead: [36]
  he mastered it! [60, 7]
The desert bloomed for him as magic [10, 18]
  garden,
where blossom devilish lovely women;
there he now lies in wait to lure our
  brothers
to shameful joy and hell's defilement: [36]
those whom he snares serve him as [18]
  master:
and many fell in foul disaster. [36, 7]
When Titurel, bowed down with age and
  stricken,
to his son dominion had given, [25]
Amfortas planned without delay [53]
to end this plague: went on his way.
What happened you now understand: [4]
the Spear is held in Klingsor's hand; [1h, 36]
and now he uses it to wound our brothers. [4]
The Grail he covets; he hopes soon to win
  it!

unkund blieb mir, was dorten er gesündigt,
doch wollt er büssen nun, ja heilig werden!
Ohnmächtig, in sich selbst die Sünde zu
  ertöten,
an sich legt er die Frevlerhand,
die nun dem Grale zugewandt,
verachtungsvoll des Hüter von sich stiess.
Darob die Wut nun Klingsorn unterwies,

wie seines schmähl'chen Opfers Tat
ihm gäbe zu bösem Zauber Rat:
  den fand er nun.
Die Wüste schuf er sich zum Wonnegarten,

drin wachsen teuflisch holde Frauen;
dort will des Grales Ritter er erwarten

zu böser Lust und Höllengrauen:
wen er verlockt, hat er erworben:

schon viele hat er uns verdorben.
Da Titurel, in hohen Alters Mühen,

dem Sohn die Herrschaft hier verliehen
Amfortas liess es da nicht ruhn,
  der Zauberplag Einhalt zu tun.
Das wisst ihr, wie es dort sich fand:
der Speer ist nun in Klingsors Hand;
kann er selbst Heilige mit dem verwunden,
den Gral auch wähnt er fest schon uns
  entwunden!

Kundry has been turning back and forth in furious agitation. [7, 1h]

FOURTH SQUIRE

Then first of all the Spear we must reclaim!

Vor allem nun: der Speer kehr uns zurück!

THIRD SQUIRE

Ha! Who does that wins lasting joy and
  fame!

Ha! Wer ihn brächt, ihm wär's zu Ruhm
  und Glück!

GURNEMANZ

Before the ravished sanctuary [60, 25]
in fervent prayer lay Amfortas, [8]
a sign of pardon he entreated: [1e]
the Grail was lighted by a mystic [60]
  radiance;
a holy vision then appeared to him and [25]
  spoke,
these words of mystic meaning shone [1a]
  before him:
    "Made wise through pity, [54]
    the blameless fool,
    wait for him,
    the one I choose."

Vor dem verwaisten Heiligtum
in brüntst'gem Beten lag Amfortas,
ein Rettungszeichen bang erflehend:
ein sel'ger Schimmer da entfloss dem
  Grale;
ein heilig Traumgesicht nun deutlich zu
  ihm spricht
durch hell erschauter Wortezeichen Male:
    "Durch Mitleid wissend,
    der reine Tor,
    harre sein,
    den ich erkor."

THE FOUR SQUIRES
(deeply moved)

    "Made wise through pity, [54]
    the blameless fool —"

    "Durch Mitleid wissend,
    der reine Tor —"

*From the lake are heard shouts and cries from the knights and squires. Gurnemanz and the
four squires start up and turn in alarm.* [57, 22, 56]

Woe! Woe!   Weh! Weh!

KNIGHTS

Hoho!   Hoho!

SQUIRES

Ah!   Auf!

KNIGHTS

Who dared to do it?   Wer ist der Frevler?

A wild swan flutters unsteadily from over the lake.

GURNEMANZ

What is it?   Was gibt's?

FOURTH SQUIRE

There!   Dort!

THIRD SQUIRE

Here!   Hier!

SECOND SQUIRE

A swan!   Ein Schwan!

FOURTH SQUIRE

A forest swan!   Ein wilder Schwan!

THIRD SQUIRE

And it is wounded!   [10]   Er ist verwundet!

ALL KNIGHTS AND SQUIRES

Ha! Shameful! Shameful!   Ha, wehe! Wehe!

GURNEMANZ

Who shot the swan?   Wer schoss den Schwan?

The swan, after a laboured flight, falls to the ground exhausted; the second knight draws an arrow from its breast.

FIRST KNIGHT

The King had hailed it as a happy omen [22]   Der König grüsste ihn als gutes Zeichen,
as o'er the lake circled the swan,   als überm See kreiste der Schwan,
and then a shaft...   da flog ein Pfeil...

Knights and squires lead in Parsifal.

KNIGHTS

He it was!   Der war's!

SQUIRES

He shot!   Der schoss!
See his bow there!   Dies der Bogen!

(indicating Parsifal's bow)

SECOND KNIGHT
(producing the arrow)

And the arrow is just like his.   Hier der Pfeil, den seinen gleich.

GURNEMANZ
(to Parsifal)

Did you deal to our swan his death-blow? [56]   Bist du's, der diesen Schwan erlegte?

PARSIFAL

Of course! I shoot at all things that fly! [57]   Gewiss! Im Fluge treff ich, was fliegt!

92

You killed the swan?   Du tatest das?
And feel no horror at the crime?   [56]   Und bangt es dich nicht vor der Tat?

SQUIRES AND KNIGHTS

Punish the culprit!   [10]   Strafe den Frevler!

GURNEMANZ

Shameful, cruel deed!   Unerhörtes Werk!
So you can murder, here, within this forest,   Du konntest morden, hier, im heil'gen Walde,
where quiet, holy peace should reign?   des stiller Friede dich umfing?
The woodland creatures, are they not   [11]   Des Haines Tiere nahten dir nicht zahm?
your friends?
Are they not gentle and tame?   Grüssten dich freundlich und fromm?
From the branches the birds sang their   [40]   Aus den Zweigen was sangen die Vöglein
songs to you.   dir?
What harm did the faithful swan?   Was tat dir der treue Schwan?
His mate he was seeking, so they both   [22]   Sein Weibchen zu suchen flog der auf,
might fly and circle over the lake,   mit ihm zu kreisen über den See,
thus nobly consecrating the bath.   [25]   den so er herrlich weihte zum Bad.
Were you not amazed?   Dem stauntest du nicht?
No, all you did was loose a cruel shaft   [57]   Dich lockt'es nur zu wild kindischem
from your bow.   Bogengeschoss?
He was our friend: what is he to you?   [3x]   Er war uns hold: was ist er nun dir?
Gurnemanz kneels down by the swan.
Here, look here! 'twas here you struck,   Hier, schau her! hier, trafst du ihn,
his blood not yet dry, limp, drooping his   da starrt noch das Blut, matt hängen die
wings now,   Flügel,
his snowy plumage darkened and stained,   das Schneegefieder dunkel befleckt,
and broken his eye, see how he looks!   gebrochen das Aug, siehst du den Blick?
*Parsifal has followed Gurnemanz with growing emotion, now he breaks his bow and hurls
his arrows away. [56, 57, 3x]*
Do you regret an act so heartless?   Wirst deiner Sündentat du inne?
Parsifal passes his hand over his eyes.
Speak, boy, do you repent your cruel deed?   [1e]   Sag, Knab, erkennst du deine grosse
       Schuld?
How could you commit this crime?   Wie konntest du sie begehn?

PARSIFAL

I did not know then.   [43]   Ich wusste sie nicht.

GURNEMANZ

Where are you from?   [57]   Wo bist du her?

PARSIFAL

I do not know.   Das weiss ich nicht.

GURNEMANZ

Who is your father?   Wer ist dein Vater?

PARSIFAL

I do not know.   [1e]   Das weiss ich nicht.

GURNEMANZ

Who sent you to seek this forest?   Wer sandte dich dieses Weges?

PARSIFAL

I do not know.   [43]   Das weiss ich nicht.

GURNEMANZ

What name have you?   Dein Name denn?

PARSIFAL

I once had many, [58]   Ich hatte viele,
but now those names are all forgot.   doch weiss ich ihrer keinen mehr.

GURNEMANZ

There's nothing that you know?   [57]   Das weiss du alles nicht?
                  (aside)
            Then one so dull   So dumm wie den
I've never met — save Kundry here!   erfand bisher ich Kundry nur!
(to the squires, who have assembled in increasing numbers)
            Be off!   Jetzt geht!
The King requires your attendance there! [45]   Versäumt den König im Bade nicht!
Go!   Helft!
The squires reverently lift the dead swan onto a bier of fresh branches and move away with it
towards the lake. [45, 22] At length only Gurnemanz, Parsifal and — apart — Kundry remain
behind. Gurnemanz turns back to Parsifal. [25, 22, 58]
Now speak: you cannot answer my   Nun sag: nichts weisst du was ich dich
     questions: frage;
     but tell what you can,   jetzt meld, was du weisst;
     for something you must remember.   denn etwas musst du doch wissen.

PARSIFAL

I have a mother, Herzeleide her name!   [58]   Ich hab eine Mutter, Herzeleide sie heisst!
In woods and in lonely meadows we made   [57]   Im Wald und auf wilder Aue waren wir
     our home.   heim.

GURNEMANZ

Who gave you your weapons?   Wer gab dir den Bogen?

PARSIFAL

            I made them myself   Den schuf ich mir selbst
to fright the savage eagles from the   vom Forst die wilden Adler zu
     forest.   verscheuchen.

GURNEMANZ

An eagle you seem yourself, and nobly   Doch adelig scheinst du doch selbst und
     born too;   hochgeboren,
why did your mother not find you   warum nicht liess deine Mutter
     worthier weapons to handle?   [57]   bessere Waffen dich lehren?

Parsifal is silent.

KUNDRY
(who during Gurnemanz's recital of the fate of Amfortas has been violently writhing in furious
agitation, now, still lying in the undergrowth, eyes Parsifal keenly and, as he is silent, hoarsely
calls:)

All fatherless did his mother bear him,   Den Vaterlosen gebar die Mutter,
for in battle slain was Gamuret!   [58]   als im Kampf erschlagen Gamuret!
To save her son from dying   Vor gleichem frühen Heldentod
as his father perished, far from arms   den Sohn zu wahren, waffenfremd
and people, as simple fool she raised him: [54]   in Öden erzog sie ihn zum Toren:
     more fool she.   [36]   die Törin.

She laughs.

PARSIFAL
(who has listened to her with sudden attention)

Yes! And once I saw a glittering array   [59]   Ja! Und einst am Waldessaume vorbei,
     of men on noble horses   auf schönen Tieren sitzend,
     pass the edge of the forest;   kamen glänzende Männer;
I wanted to be like them: ihnen wollt ich gleichen:
     but laughing they galloped away.   sie lachten und jagten davon.
So I pursued, but I could not overtake [57]   Nun lief ich nach, doch konnt ich sie nicht
     them;   erreichen;
     through savage places passing, over [59]   durch Wildnisse kam ich, bergauf, talab;
     hill and dale;

night followed day, day followed night:
my bow and arrows defended me
when the beasts or men attacked
me . . .

Kundry has risen and moved towards the men.

KUNDRY

Yes! Robbers and giants fell to his might,
the fearless boy soon taught them to fear [57]
him.

PARSIFAL
(*in surprise*)

Who fears me? Say!

KUNDRY

The wicked!

PARSIFAL

So those who fought me, were they wicked? [5]
Gurnemanz laughs.
Who is good? [60]

GURNEMANZ
(*serious again*)

Your dear mother, whom you deserted, [58a]
and who for you now must mourn and
grieve.

KUNDRY

She grieves no more: for his mother is [5]
dead.

PARSIFAL
(*in fearful alarm*)

Dead? My mother? Who says so? [36]

KUNDRY

As I rode by I saw her dying: [5]
and, fool, she sent you her greeting.

Parsifal springs furiously at Kundry and seizes her by the throat. Gurnemanz restrains him.
[57]

GURNEMANZ

So wild and violent! Brutal again?
After Gurnemanz has freed Kundry, Parsifal stands as if dazed. [42, 58]
What harm has she done? She tells the
truth,
for Kundry sees much and never lies.

PARSIFAL
(*seized with violent trembling*)

I am fainting!

Kundry, seeing Parsifal's condition, at once hastens to a spring in the wood and now brings water in a horn, sprinkles Parsifal with it and then gives it to him to drink. [23, 36]

GURNEMANZ

Right so! That is the Grail's compassion: [26]
the evil ends when with good it's
returned.

KUNDRY
(*gloomily*)

Good I do never: for rest I'm yearning, [52b]

oft ward es Nacht, dann wieder Tag:
mein Bogen musste mir frommen
gegen Wild und grosse Männer . . .

KUNDRY

Ja! Schächer und Riesen traf seine Kraft;
den freislichen Knaben lernten sie
fürchten.

PARSIFAL

Wer fürchtet mich? Sag!

KUNDRY

Die Bösen!

PARSIFAL

Die mich bedrohten, waren sie bös?

Wer ist gut?

GURNEMANZ

Deine Mutter, der du entlaufen,
und die um dich sich nun härmt und
grämt.

KUNDRY

Zu End ihr Gram: seine Mutter ist tot.

PARSIFAL

Tot? Meine Mutter? Wer sagt's?

KUNDRY

Ich ritt vorbei und sah sie sterben:
dich Toren hiess sie mich grüssen.

GURNEMANZ

Verrückter Knabe! Wieder Gewalt?

Was tat dir das Weib? Es sagte wahr;

denn nie lügt Kundry, doch sah sie viel.

PARSIFAL

Ich verschmachte!

GURNEMANZ

So recht! So nach des Grales Gnade:
das Böse bannt, wer's mit Gutem vergilt.

KUNDRY

Nie tu ich Gutes: nur Ruhe will ich,

I'm yearning, ah! I'm weary. [4]	nur Ruhe, ach! der Müden.

She turns away sadly and, while Gurnemanz tends Parsifal in a fatherly way, she creeps, unobserved by them, towards a thicket in the wood.

Slumber! Oh, may I not be wakened!	Schlafen! O, da mich keiner wecke!

(starting in fear)

No! Not slumber! Terrors seize me! [36]	Nein! Nicht schlafen! Grausen fasst mich!

She falls into a violent trembling, then lets her arms and head drop wearily. [4, 7]

Vain to resist! The time has come. [7]	Machtlose Wehr! Die Zeit ist da.

By the lake there is movement, and at length in the background the procession of knights and squires returning home with Amfortas's litter.

Slumber — slumber — I must! [4]	Schlafen — schlafen — ich muss!

She sinks down behind the bushes and is not seen further.

GURNEMANZ

But from the lake the King returns; [29]	Vom Bade kehrt der König heim;
the sun is high now: [25]	hoch steht die Sonne:
so to our celebration let me lead you.	nun lass zum frommen Mahle mich dich geleiten,
If you are pure,	denn bist du rein,
then now the Grail will comfort and	wird nun der Gral dich tränken und
refresh you.	speisen.

He has gently put Parsifal's arm round his neck and supporting him in this way he leads him with very slow steps. Very gradually, the scene begins to change.

PARSIFAL

Who is the Grail? [25]	Wer ist der Gral?

GURNEMANZ

That can't be told;	Das sagt sich nicht;
but if to serve it you are bidden,	doch, du selbst zu ihm erkoren,
that knowledge long will not be hidden.	bleibt dir die Kunde unverloren.
Behold!	Und sieh!
I think I know you now indeed: [29]	Mich dünkt, dass ich dich recht erkannt:
no pathway to the Grail doth lead,	kein Weg führt zu ihm durch das Land,
and none can venture to approach it	und niemand könnte ihn beschreiten,
unless the Grail itself has called him.	den er nicht selber möcht geleiten.

PARSIFAL

I scarcely stir,	Ich schreite kaum,
yet all things move apace.	doch wähn ich mich schon weit.

GURNEMANZ

You see, my son,	Du siehst, mein Sohn,
here Time is one with Space.	zum Raum wird hier die Zeit.

Gradually, while Gurnemanz and Parsifal appear to walk, the scene changes more perceptibly: the woods disappear and in the rocky walls a gateway opens, which closes behind them. [39, 25, 41, 50, 1a, 30] The way has led upwards through walls of rock, and the scene has entirely changed. Gurnemanz and Parsifal now enter the mighty hall of the castle of the Grail. Gurnemanz turns to Parsifal, who stands as if bewitched.

Now pay good heed, and let me see: [29]	Nun achte wohl, und lass mich sehn:
if you're a fool and pure,	bist du ein Tor und rein,
what wisdom here your folly may secure.	welch Wissen dir auch mag beschieden sein.

Scene Two. *A pillared hall with a vaulted dome over the Feast-chamber. On both sides at the far end the doors are opened; the knights of the Grail enter from the right and range themselves by the Feast-tables. [25, 30]*

KNIGHTS OF THE GRAIL

O Feast of Love undying,	Zum letzten Liebesmahle
from day to day renewed,	gerüstet Tag für Tag,

A procession of squires passes rapidly across the backstage.

draw near, as for the last time,	gleich ob zum letzten Male
to taste this sacred food.	es heut uns letzten mag,

A second procession of squires crosses the hall.

Who revels in good deeds	wer guter Tat sich freut,
this holy Feast still feeds:	ihm wird das Mahl erneut:
he dares approach the shrine	der Labung darf er nahn,
to share this gift divine.	die hehrste Gab empfahn.

The assembled knights station themselves at the tables. From the left door Amfortas is borne in on a litter by squires and serving brothers; before him walk the four squires bearing the covered shrine of the Grail. This procession moves to the centre backstage, where there is a raised couch on which Amfortas is set down from the litter; before it is an oblong stone altar on which the squires place the covered shrine of the Grail. [41, 29, 25]

YOUTHS
(from halfway up the dome)

For sins of the world	Den sündigen Welten,
with thousand sorrows	mit tausend Schmerzen,
His sacred blood He offered;	wie einst sein Blut geflossen,
to the world's Redeemer	dem Erlösungshelden
with joyful heart,	sei nun mit freudigem Herzen
oh, how gladly my blood I proffer:	mein Blut vergossen:
He died, for sin atoning thus,	der Leib, den Er zur Süh'n uns bot,
He lives, by death He lives in us!	er lebt in uns durch seinen Tod!

BOYS
(from the summit of the dome)

In faith and love,	[11]	Der Glaube lebt,
behold the dove,		die Taube schwebt,
the Saviour's shining token:		des Heilands holder Bote:
take ye the wine,		der für euch fliesst,
His blood divine,		des Weines geniesst,
and bread of life here broken!		und nehmt von Lebens-Brote!

When all have taken their places, and after a complete silence, the voice of the aged Titurel is heard in the extreme background from a vaulted niche behind Amfortas's couch, as if from a tomb.

TITUREL

My son Amfortas, are you prepared?	Mein Sohn Amfortas, bist du am Amt?

(silence)

Shall I the Grail see once again and live still?	Soll ich den Gral heut noch erschaun und leben?

(silence)

Must I die then, without its light to guide me?	[46]	Muss ich sterben, vom Retter ungeleitet?

AMFORTAS
(in an outburst of painful desperation)

Sorrow! Oh, eternal grief!	[41]	Wehe! Wehe mir der Qual!
My father, oh! just once more	[46]	Mein Vater, oh! noch einmal
resume the sacred task!		verrichte du das Amt!
Live, live and let me perish.		Lebe, leb und lass mich sterben.

TITUREL

Entombed I live here by our Saviour's grace;	[46, 25]	Im Grabe leb ich durch des Heilands Huld:
too weak, however, now to serve Him.		zu schwach doch bin ich ihm zu dienen.
You make atonement for your guilt!		Du büss im Dienste deine Schuld!
Reveal the Grail!		Enthüllet den Gral!

AMFORTAS
(restraining the squires)

No! Leave it unrevealed! Oh!	[46, 36]	Nein! Lasst ihn unenthüllt! O!
May no one, no one know the burning pain		Dass keiner, keiner diese Qual ermisst,
caused by the holy sight that gives you delight!		die mir der Anblick weckt, der euch entzückt!

What is the Spear-wound, all its raging smart,
compared to the pain, the agony
of being condemned to serve this task!
Woeful my birth-right, defiled by [46]
sinning;
I, only sinner, am the guardian
who holds the Grail for sinless others, [25]
entreating its holy blessing on my brothers! [36]
Chastisement! Merciless chastisement [41]
from, ah! the offended God of mercy! [36]
For Him, for His all-holy greeting, [25]
my stricken heart is yearning;
in deepest innermost repentance, [41]
for Him my soul is burning.
The time is near:
a light beam sinks upon the holiest shrine: [25]

the covering falls.
The blood within that pure holiest Cup [1a, e]
now glows and shines with tender light.
Transfixed by rapturous and joyful pain,

the fount of that holy blood,
I feel it flowing in my heart: [1i]
the furious surge of my own guilty [45]
blood,
my vile blood now defiled
by shame, recoils before it;
to the world of sin and lust [4]
how wildly now it is gushing.
The wound has opened again, [1e]
my blood now is streaming forth,
here, through the spear-wound, a
wound like His,
inflicted by the Spear that wounded
Him,
the Spear that inflicted the sacred wound, [41]
through which with bleeding tears
the Holy One wept for the sins of man,

in pity's holiest yearning.
And now here from me, in my sacred [25]
office,
the guardian of godliest treasure,
of redemption's balm the keeper,
my fevered sinful blood flows forth, [36, 4]
ever renewed by the tide of yearning [7x]
that, ah! no repentance ever stills!
Have mercy! Have mercy! [36, 34a, b]
All-merciful! Ah, have mercy! [3]
Take back my birth-right,
end my affliction,
that holy I perish —
pure, whole, and healed! [9]

Was ist die Wunde, ihrer Schmerzen Wut

gegen die Not, die Höllenpein,
zu diesem Amt verdammt zu sein!
Wehvolles Erbe, dem ich verfallen

ich einz'ger Sünder unter allen,
des höchsten Heiligtums zu pflegen
auf Reine herab zu flehen seinen Segen!
O Strafe! Strafe ohne gleichen
des, ach! gekränkten Gnadenreichen!
Nach Ihm, nach seinem Weihegrüsse,
muss sehnlich mich's verlangen;
aus tiefster Seele Heilesbusse
zu Ihm muss ich gelangen.
Die Stunde naht:
ein Lichtstrahl senkt sich auf das heilige
Werk:
die Hülle fällt.
Des Weihegefässes göttlicher Gehalt
erglüht mit leuchtender Gewalt;
durchzückt von seligsten Genusses
Schmerz,
des heiligsten Blutes Quell
fühl ich sich giessen in mein Herz:
des eignen sündigen Blutes Gewell,

in wahnsinniger Flucht
muss mir zurück dann fliessen,
in die Welt der Sünden sucht
mit wilder Scheu sich ergiessen;
von neuem sprengt es das Tor
daraus es nun strömt hervor,
hier durch die Wunde, der seinen gleich,

geschlagen von desselben Speeres
Streich,
der dort dem Erlöser die Wunde stach,
aus der mit blut'gen Tränen
der Göttliche weint' ob der Menschheit
Schmach
in Mitleids heiligem Sehnen,
und aus der nun mir, an heiligster Stelle,

dem Pfleger göttlichster Güter,
des Erlösungsbalsams Hüter,
das heisse Sündenblut entquillt,
ewig erneut aus des Sehnens Quelle,
das, ach! keine Büssung je mir stillt!
Erbarmen! Erbarmen!
Du Allerbarmer! Ach, Erbarmen!
Nimm mir mein Erbe,
schliesse die Wunde,
dass heilig ich sterbe,
rein — Dir gesunde!

He sinks back as if unconscious.

BOYS AND YOUTHS
(*from halfway up the dome*)

"Made wise through pity, [54]
the blameless fool:
wait for him,
the one I choose."

"Durch Mitleid wissend,
der reine Tor:
harre sein,
den ich erkor!"

So truly you were promised: wait on in hope, fulfil your task today!	[25]	So ward es dir verhiessen: harre getrost, des Amtes walte heut!

TITUREL

Reveal now the Grail! Enthüllet den Gral!

Amfortas raises himself slowly and with difficulty. The acolytes remove the cover from the golden shrine and take from it an antique crystal chalice, from which they also remove a covering, and place it before Amfortas. [1f, e, h]

YOUTHS' VOICES
(from on high)

"Take my body and eat, take and drink my blood, in holy, loving token!	[1]	"Nehmet hin meinen Leib, nehmet hin mein Blut, um unsrer Liebe willen!"

While Amfortas bows devoutly in silent prayer before the chalice, a dusky glimmer envelopes the hall.

BOYS
(from the summit)

"Take and drink my blood, take my body and eat, as a remembrance of me."	[1]	"Nehmet hin mein Blut, nehmet hin meinen Leib, auf dass ihr mein gedenkt!"

Here a dazzling ray of light falls from above on the crystal cup, which now glows ever more intensely in a brilliant crimson, shedding a soft light on everything around. Amfortas, transfigured, raises the Grail aloft and waves it gently round to every side, consecrating the bread and wine. All are kneeling. [3, 41, 50]

TITUREL

O holiest rapture! How radiant God's greeting today!	[1a, 25]	O! heilige Wonne, wie hell grüsst uns heute der Herr!

Amfortas sets down the Grail again, and its glow gradually fades as the darkness lightens: at this the acolytes replace the vessel in the shrine and cover it as before. [8, 25] *Daylight returns.* [30]

BOYS
(from the summit)

Wine and bread of that Last Supper, changed by Him, the Lord of mercy, through the saving might of love into blood, which He then shed, into flesh, which men then broke!	Wein und Brot des letzten Mahles wandelt' einst der Herr des Grales, durch des Mitleids Liebesmacht in das Blut, das er vergoss, in den Leib, den dar er bracht!

Meanwhile, the four squires, after closing the shrine, take from the altar table the two wine flagons and two baskets of bread, which Amfortas had previously blessed by passing the chalice of the Grail over them, distribute the bread among the knights and fill with wine the cups standing before them. The knights seat themselves at the Feast, as does Gurnemanz, who has kept a place empty beside him and signals to Parsifal to come and partake of the meal. Parsifal, however, remains standing apart, motionless and silent, as if completely transported.

YOUTHS' VOICES
(from on high)

Blood and body, gift of Heaven, changed today for your salvation, in our sacred Feast of Love, to the wine filling your cup, to the bread that now you eat.	Blut und Leib der heil'gen Gabe wandelt heut' zu eurer Labe sel'ger Tröstung Liebesgeist in den Wein, der euch nun floss, in das Brot, das heut' ihr speis't.

THE KNIGHTS
(first group)

Take ye the bread, change it anew	Nehmet vom Brot, wandelt es kühn

to manly strength and valour,		in Leibes Kraft und Stärke,
brave unto death,		treu bis zum Tod,
steadfast and true		fest jedem Müh'n
to work here the highest will of Heaven!		zu wirken des Heilands Werke!

THE KNIGHTS
(second group)

Take ye the wine,		Nehmet vom Wein,
change it anew		wandelt ihn neu
to fiery blood in you burning,		zu Lebens feurigem Blute,
banded as one,		froh im Verein,
brothers and true		brudergetreu
to fight on with courage unfailing!		zu kämpfen mit seligem Mute!

ALL KNIGHTS

Blessed in faith	[25]	Selig im Glauben
and in loving!		und Liebe!

YOUTHS AND BOYS

Blessed in loving!		Selig in Liebe!
Blessed in faith!		Selig im Glauben!

The knights rise and walk from each side to the centre, where they solemnly embrace. Amfortas, who has taken no part in the meal, has gradually sunk down from his state of inspired exaltation; he bows his head, and presses his hand to his wound. The squires approach him, and their movements show that the wound has broken out afresh; they attend to it, and assist their master back to the litter. Then, while all are preparing to leave, they bear out Amfortas and the holy shrine in the order in which they came. The knights likewise fall into solemn procession and slowly leave the hall. The procession with Amfortas disappears entirely. The light diminishes. Squires pass quickly through the hall. The last knights and squires have now left the hall, and the doors are closed. Parsifal still stands stiff and motionless; on hearing Amfortas' cry of agony, he had pressed his hand suddenly and convulsively to his heart, remaining long in that position. [25, 11, 41, 29, 42, 54, 30]

GURNEMANZ
(coming up to Parsifal in an ill humour and shaking him by the arm)

You're still standing there?	[54]	Was stehst du noch da?
Know you what you saw?		Weisst du, was du sah'st?

Parsifal presses his heart convulsively and shakes his head. [3x] *Gurnemanz is much irritated.*

So you are nothing but a fool!	[54]	Du bist doch eben nur ein Tor!

He opens a small side door.

Off with you, on your way again!	[57]	Dort hinaus, deinem Wege zu!
And hark to Gurnemanz:		Doch rät dir Gurnemanz:
henceforth leave our swans in peace:	[22]	lass' du hier künftig die Schwäne in Ruh'
go seeking — you gander — for geese!		und suche dir Gänser die Gans!

He pushes Parsifal out and bangs the door angrily upon him. While he follows the knights, upon the last bar the curtain closes. [54]

AN ALTO VOICE
(from on high)

"Made wise through pity,	[54]	"Durch Mitleid wissend
the blameless fool."		der reine Tor."

VOICES
(from the mid-height and the summit)

Blessed in loving!	[25]	Selig im Glauben!

Bells. [30]

Act Two

[7, 41x, 36]

Klingsor's magic castle. In the inner keep of a tower which is open to the sky. Stone steps lead up to the battlements and down into the darkness below the stage which represents the rampart. Magical and necromantic apparatus. Klingsor on the offset of the tower to one side, sitting before a metal mirror. [4]

KLINGSOR

The time is come.		Die Zeit ist da.
The fool's attracted by my castle,	[54, 57]	Schon lockt mein Zauberschloss den Toren,
with childish laughter he's approaching me!		den, kindisch jauchzend, fern ich nahen seh!
In deathly slumber held by curse she lies,	[4, 36]	Im Todesschlafe hält der Fluch sie fest,
but by my spells I'll waken her.		der ich den Krampf zu lösen weiss.
Up then! To work!		Auf denn! An's Werk!

He moves down towards the centre and lights incense, which immediately fills the background with blue smoke. He then seats himself again before his magical instruments, and calls with strange gestures into the depths below. [4]

Arise! Arise! To me!		Herauf! Herauf! Zu mir!
Your master calls you, nameless woman,	[7]	Dein Meister ruft dich Namenlose,
first she-devil! Rose of Hades!		Urteufelin! Höllenrose!
Herodias were you, and what else?		Herodias war'st du, und was noch?
Gundryggia then, Kundry here!	[4]	Gundryggia dort, Kundry hier!
Come here! Come here now, Kundry!	[7]	Hieher! Hieher denn, Kundry!
Your master calls: arise!	[61]	Dein Meister ruft: herauf!

In the blue light Kundry's figure rises up. She seems asleep. She moves like one awaking. Finally she utters a terrible cry. [41x, 4, 60, 36, 34c]

Awake now? Ha!		Erwachst du? Ha!
To my spell again		Meinem Banne wieder
you surrender now, in time of need.		verfallen heut' — zur rechten Zeit.

Kundry gives a loud wail of misery that sinks gradually into low accents of fear.

Say, where have you been roaming again?		Sag! wo trieb'st du dich wieder umher?
Fie! There with that rabble of knights	[60]	Pfui! Dort bei dem Rittergesipp,
though like a beast they have treated you!		wo wie ein Vieh du dich halten lässt!
With me don't you fare much better?		Gefällt dir's bei mir nicht besser?
And when for me you conquered their leader —	[36]	Als ihren Meister du mir gefangen —
ha ha! — the Grail's most holy defender,	[41y]	ha ha! den reinen Hüter des Grales,
what drove you to seek them again?		was jagte dich da wieder fort?

KUNDRY
(hoarsely and brokenly, as though striving to regain speech)

Ah! — Ah!	[43]	Ach! — Ach!
Deepest night...	[4]	Tiefe Nacht...
Madness... Oh! — Rage...		Wahnsinn... Oh! — Wut...
Ah! Sorrow!	[43, 10]	Ach! Jammer!
Sleep... sleep...	[9]	Schlaf... Schlaf...
deepest sleep... death!		tiefer Schlaf... Tod!

KLINGSOR

Has someone else aroused you? Hey?	Da weckte dich ein And'rer? He?

KUNDRY
(as before)

Yes... my curse.	[36]	Ja... mein Fluch.
Oh! Yearning... yearning!	[41]	Oh! Sehnen... Sehnen!

KLINGSOR

Ha ha! So for the knights you're yearning?	Ha ha! dort nach den keuschen Rittern?

There ... I ... served them.   [37]   Da ... da ... dient ich.

KLINGSOR

Yes, yes, atoning for the evil   Ja, ja, den Schaden zu vergüten,
  that you had maliciously wrought?   [42]   den du ihnen böslich gebracht?
  But they cannot help;   Sie helfen dir nicht;
  all can be purchased,   feil sind sie Alle
  when I provide the price: biet' ich den rechten Preis:
  the strongest will fall,   der festeste fällt,
  sinking in your embraces,   [43]   sinkt er dir in die Arme,
  and so he falls by the Spear   und so verfällt er dem Speer,
  that from their king himself I have [1h, 7, 42]   den ihrem Meister selbst ich entwandt. —
  seized.
The most dangerous of all today must be   [54]   Den Gefährlichsten gilt's nun heut' zu
  met: besteh'n:
  his folly shields him well.   ihn schirmt der Torheit Schild.

KUNDRY

I — will not. — Oh ... oh! ...   [3x, 42, 9] Ich — will nicht. — Oh ... oh! ...

KLINGSOR

You'll do it, for you must.   [37]   Wohl willst du, denn du musst.

KUNDRY

You ... cannot ... compel me.   [37]   Du ... kannst mich ... nicht ... halten.

KLINGSOR

But I can force you.   Aber dich fassen.

KUNDRY

You? ...   Du? ...

KLINGSOR

Your master. [61, 37]   Dein Meister.

KUNDRY

And by what power?   Aus welcher Macht?

KLINGSOR

Ha! — Because I'm immune   [36]   Ha! — Weil einzig an mir
from your power — I alone.   deine Macht nichts vermag.

KUNDRY
(*with a shrill laugh*)

Ha ha! Are you chaste?   [37]   Ha ha! Bist du keusch?

KLINGSOR
(*furiously*)

Why ask me that, accursed witch?   [37, 34d] Was fräg'st du das, verfluchtes Weib?
  Fearful my fate!   Furchtbare Not!
So I am derided now,   So lacht nun der Teufel mein,
because once to be holy I strove?   [4]   dass einst ich nach dem Heiligen rang?
  Fearful my fate!   [41x]   Furchtbare Not!
Fiery longings and scorching pain,   [7]   Ungebändigten Sehnens Pein,
hellish desires and pangs of lust,   schrecklichster Triebe Höllendrang,
which I once stifled at fearful cost,   den ich zum Todesschweigen mir zwang,
rise to mock me aloud   [34d]   lacht und höhnt er nun laut
through you, you devil's bride!   [36]   durch dich, des Teufels Braut?
  Ha! — beware!   Hüte dich!
One for his scorn and contempt pays dearly, [7] Hohn und Verachtung büsste schon
                                           Einer,

102

that proud one, strong in holiness,
who drove me from his side:
his son has fallen; [45]
unredeemed
shall that holiest guardian now languish, [25]
and soon, I'm certain,
I shall possess the Grail. [41x]
Ha ha! [45]
Was he to your taste, Amfortas the brave,
whom I procured for your delight? [36]

der Stolze stark in Heiligkeit,
der einst mich von sich stiess:
sein Stamm verfiel mir,
unerlös't
soll der Heiligen Hüter mir schmachten,
und bald, so wähn' ich,
hüt' ich mir selbst den Gral.
Ha ha!
Gefiel er dir wohl, Amfortas der Held,
den ich zur Wonne dir gesellt?

KUNDRY

Oh! Sorrow! Sorrow! [42, 37]
Weak even he, — weak all men! [34a]
I'm accursed and I [41x, 36]
bring all to ruin!
Oh, never-ending sleep, [41x]
only release,
how, — how can I find it?

O! Jammer! Jammer!
Schwach auch er, — schwach alle,
meinem Fluche mit mir
alle verfallen!
O ewiger Schlaf,
einziges Heil,
wie, — wie dich gewinnen?

KLINGSOR

Ha! One who spurns you can set you free: [54]
so try with the boy drawing near!

Ha! Wer dich trotzte, lös'te dich frei:
versuch's mit dem Knaben, der nah't!

KUNDRY

I will not!

Ich will nicht!

KLINGSOR
(*hastily mounting the tower wall*)

See him, he's scaling the wall. [57]

Jetzt schon erklimmt er die Burg.

KUNDRY

Oh! Sorrow! Sorrow! [34a]
Is that why I wakened?
Must I? Ah! [36]

O! Wehe! Wehe!
Erwachte ich darum?
Muss ich? Muss?

KLINGSOR
(*looking out*)

Ha! He is fair, he's handsome! [43]

Ha! Er ist schön, der Knabe!

KUNDRY

Oh! — Oh! — Ah! What grief! [36]

O! — O! — Wehe mir!

Klingsor, leaning out, blows a horn.

KLINGSOR

Ho! You watchmen! Ho! Warriors! [59]
Heroes! Up! Foes are near!
Ha! How they rush to the ramparts,
my deluded band of warriors,
defending their beautiful witches!
So! — Courage! Courage!
Ha ha! But he's not afraid:
from bold Sir Ferris he's wrested a
weapon,
and fights with it fiercely, braving them
all.

Ho! Ihr Wächter! Ho! Ritter!
Helden! Auf! Feinde nah'
Ha! Wie zur Mauer sie stürmen,
die betörten Eigenholde,
zum Schutz ihres schönen Geteufels!
So! — Mutig! Mutig!
Ha ha! Der fürchtet sich nicht:
dem Helden Ferris entwand er die Waffe,
die führt er nun freislich wider den
Schwarm.

Kundry falls into wild hysterical laughter, which ends in a woeful moan.

How feebly those dull ones resist his
attack!
Some struck in the thigh, others in the
shoulder!
Ha ha! They're yielding! They're [36, 57]
fleeing!

Wie übel den Tölpeln der Eifer gedeih't!
Dem schlug er den Arm, jenem den
Schenkel!
Ha ha! Sie weichen! Sie fliehen!

The blue light is extinguished and all is dark below, in contrast to the bright blue sky over the walls.

103

Sorely wounded they're running for home!	[54]	Seine Wunde trägt jeder nach heim!
What pleasure that gives me!		Wie das ich euch gönne!
Would that the whole		Möge denn so
despised assembly of knights		das ganze Rittergezücht
thus might destroy one another!	[57]	unter sich selber sich würgen!
Ha! How proudly he stands on the rampart!		Ha! Wie stolz er nun steht auf der Zinne!
He's laughing, and flushed with his victory,		Wie lachen ihm die Rosen der Wangen,
with childish surprise		da kindisch erstaunt
sees deserted the garden below!	[39]	in den einsamen Garten er blickt!

He turns towards the back.

Hey! Kundry!	[34a]	He! Kundry!

(not perceiving her)

Ha? At your work?	[36]	Wie? Schon am Werk?
Ha ha! The magic spell I know	[58]	Ha ha! Den Zauber wusst' ich wohl,
that always compels you to serve my	[7]	der immer dich wieder zum Dienst mir
designs!		gesellt!

(turning outwards again)

You there, childish and free,	[54]	Du da, kindischer Spross,
though — your		was — auch
mission was foretold,		Weissagung dich wies,
so young and dull,		zu jung und dumm
you'll fall right into my hands:		fiel'st du in meine Gewalt:
when pureness once has left you,		die Reinheit dir entrissen,
then I will be your master!	[7]	bleibst mir du zugewiesen!

The whole tower rapidly sinks with him; in its place rises the magic garden. The magic garden fills the whole stage with tropical vegetation and a luxuriant growth of flowers. It rises in terraces to the extreme background, where it is bounded by the battlements of the castle. On one side appear projections of the palace building, in rich Moorish style. Upon the rampart stands Parsifal, gazing in astonishment into the garden. [57, 59] From all sides rush in the Flower-Maidens clad in light veil-like garments, first singly, then in groups, forming a confused, many-coloured throng. They seem as though just startled out of sleep.

ALL MAIDENS
(to one another)

Here they were fighting!	Hier war das Tosen!
Weapons! Wildly shouting!	Waffen! Wilde Rüfe!
Weapons! Who is the culprit?	Wehe! Wer ist der Frevler?
Where is the culprit?	Wo ist der Frevler?
We'll have vengeance!	Auf zur Rache!

1ST MAIDEN 1ST GROUP

My beloved is wounded!	[44]	Mein Geliebter verwundet!

1ST MAIDEN 2ND GROUP

Oh, where can I find him?	Wo find' ich den meinen?

2ND MAIDEN 1ST GROUP

When I woke he had left me!	Ich erwachte alleine!

ALL MAIDENS

Where have they fled to?	Wohin entfloh'n sie?

1ST MAIDEN 2ND GROUP

Where is my beloved?	Wo ist mein Geliebter?

3RD MAIDEN 1ST GROUP

Oh, where can I find him?	Wo find' ich den meinen?

2ND MAIDEN 2ND GROUP

When I woke he had left me!	Ich erwachte alleine!

1ST MAIDEN 1ST GROUP

Oh, sorrow! Sorrow!	Oh! Weh! Ach wehe!

Where are our beloveds?	Wo sind uns're Liebsten?
Inside the castle!	Drinnen im Saale!
Where are our beloveds?	Wo sind uns're Liebsten?
We saw them go in there.	Wir sah'n sie im Saale.
We saw them all bleeding and wounded.	Wir sah'n sie mit blutender Wunde.
Ah! My lover!	Wehe! Wehe!
Ah, come help me!	Auf, zur Hilfe!
And who is our foe?	Wer ist unser Feind?

They perceive Parsifal and point him out.

There — see him!	[62]	Da — steht er!
There — see him! There — there!		Da — steht er! Dort — dort!
There he stands, there he stands!		Seht ihn dort, seht ihn dort!
Where? Ha! I saw!		Wo? — Dort! Ich sah's!

1ST MAIDEN 1ST GROUP

And my Ferris' sword in his hand!	Meines Ferris Schwert in seiner Hand!

2ND MAIDEN 1ST GROUP

My beloved's blood red on the blade.	Meines Liebsten Blut hab' ich erkannt.

CHORUSES I AND II

I saw! The castle he stormed!	Ich sah's! Der stürmte die Burg!

3RD MAIDEN 2ND GROUP

And I heard the master's horn.	Ich hörte des Meisters Horn.

3RD MAIDEN 1ST GROUP AND 2ND MAIDEN 2ND GROUP

Yes, we all heard the horn.	Ja, wir hörten sein Horn.

CHORUSES I AND II

Yes, he!	Der war's!

1ST AND 3RD MAIDENS 2ND GROUP

My hero obeyed.	Mein Held lief herzu.

2ND AND 3RD MAIDENS 1ST GROUP

They all obeyed the command.	Sie kamen Alle herzu.

1ST MAIDEN 1ST GROUP

My hero obeyed.	Mein Held lief herzu.

CHORUSES I AND II

They all obeyed the command,	Sie Alle kamen, doch Jeden
but they fell to his sword!	empfing seine Wehr!
Alas! Ah! He inflicted a wound!	Oh Weh'! Weh' ihm, der sie uns schlug!

2ND MAIDEN 1ST GROUP AND MAIDENS FROM CHORUS I

He wounded my lover.	[44]	Er schlug mir den Liebsten.

1ST MAIDEN 1ST GROUP AND MAIDENS FROM THE CHORUSES

He struck at my friend.	Mir traf er den Freund.

2ND MAIDEN 2ND GROUP AND MAIDENS FROM THE CHORUSES

His sword is still bleeding!	Noch blutet die Waffe!

1ST MAIDEN 2ND GROUP AND MAIDENS FROM THE CHORUSES

My beloved's foe.	Meines Liebsten Feind.

ALL MAIDENS

Ah! You there! Alas!	Weh! Du dort! Oh Weh'!
Why inflict such a blow?	Was schuf'st du solche Not?

Accursed, accursed you must be! Verwünscht, verwünscht sollst du sein!

Parsifal leaps somewhat further into the garden. The maidens hastily retreat. Now he pauses, full of wonder. [57]

Ha! Bold one! Ha! Kühner!

1ST MAIDEN 1ST GROUP, 1ST AND 2ND MAIDENS 2ND GROUP

Dare you approach us? Wag'st du zu nahen?

2ND AND 3RD MAIDENS 1ST GROUP, 3RD MAIDEN 2ND GROUP

Why did you wound our beloveds? Was schlug'st du uns're Geliebten?

PARSIFAL

You lovely children, I was forced to smite them! Ihr schönen Kinder, musst' ich sie nicht schlagen?

For they, you fair ones, they tried to keep [39] me from you. Zu euch, ihr Holden, ja wehrten sie mir den Weg.

1ST MAIDEN 2ND GROUP

You knew we were here? [62a] Zu uns wolltest du?

1ST MAIDEN 1ST GROUP

You'd seen us before? Sah'st du uns schon?

PARSIFAL

I have never beheld a scene so bright: if I said fair, would that seem right? Noch nie sah ich solch' zieres Geschlecht: nenn' ich euch schön, dünkt euch das recht?

2ND MAIDEN 1ST GROUP

Then truly you will not harm us? [44] So willst du uns wohl nicht schlagen?

2ND MAIDEN 2ND GROUP

You will not harm us? Willst uns nicht schlagen?

PARSIFAL

I couldn't do that. Das möcht' ich nicht.

1ST MAIDEN 2ND GROUP

And yet you injured us severely — Doch Schaden schufst du uns so vielen —

2ND AND 3RD MAIDENS 1ST AND 2ND GROUPS

— grievously harmed us! Grossen und vielen!

1ST MAIDENS 1ST AND 2ND GROUPS

You wounded all our companions! Du schlugest uns're Gespielen!

ALL MAIDENS

Who'll play with us now? Wer spielt nun mit uns?

PARSIFAL

Gladly will I! Das tu' ich gern!

The maidens, passing from wonder to enjoyment, break into a merry laugh. While Parsifal steps nearer to the excited throng, the maidens of the first group and first chorus slip away unperceived to complete their flower-adornment behind the flower-hedges. [57]

CHORUS II

If you are kind — Bist du uns hold —

2ND GROUP

Why stay so far? so bleib' nicht fern! —

CHORUS II

— stay so far from us. — bleib' nicht fern von uns.

106

And if you do not chide us —   Und willst du uns nicht schelten —

2ND MAIDEN 2ND GROUP

— reward you have beside us: — wir werden dir's entgelten:

2ND GROUP
(*to one another*)

We do not play for gold.   [62a]   Wir spielen nicht um Gold.

1ST MAIDEN 2ND GROUP

But only for love's reward.   Wir spielen um Minnes Sold.

2ND MAIDEN 2ND GROUP

If you seek to console us —   Willst auf Trost du uns sinnen, —

1ST MAIDEN 2ND GROUP

— Ah, then ties of love must hold us!   — sollst den du uns abgewinnen!

The maidens of the first group and first chorus return adorned with flowers, appearing like the flowers themselves, and make a rush at Parsifal.

2ND FLOWER 1ST GROUP

Leave him for me now!   Lasset den Knaben!

1ST FLOWER 1ST GROUP

He belongs to me!   Er gehöret mir!

3RD THEN 2ND FLOWER 1ST GROUP

No! No!   Nein! Nein!

CHORUS I

No! Me!   Nein! Mir!

CHORUS II AND 2ND GROUP

Ha! The sly ones! In secret decked   Ha! die Falschen! Sie schmückten
themselves!   heimlich sich!

While the newcomers throng round Parsifal, the maidens of the second group and second chorus hastily leave the stage to adorn themselves also.

CHORUS I AND 1ST GROUP

During the following the maidens dance in a graceful childlike manner about Parsifal, caressing him gently.

Come! Come!   [18]   Komm'! Komm'!
Handsome stranger!   Holder Knabe!
For you I'll bloom now!   Lass' mich dir blühen!
Come! To delight and please you,   Komm'! Dir zur Wonn' und Labe
that is all I long for!   gilt mein minniges Mühen!

1ST FLOWER 1ST GROUP

Come, handsome stranger!   [63]   Komm', holder Knabe!

2ND AND 3RD FLOWERS 1ST GROUP

Handsome stranger!   Holder Knabe!

The second group and the second chorus return, attired like the first, and join in the play.

ALL FLOWER MAIDENS

Come! Come!   Komm'! Komm'!
Handsome stranger!   Holder Knabe!
Ah! For you I'll blossom,   Lass' mich dir erblühen,
to delight and please you,   dir zu wonniger Labe
that is my labour of love!   gilt unser minniges Müh'n!

107

(standing in the midst of the maidens in silent enjoyment)

How fragrant you are! [63] Wie duftet ihr hold!
Are you then blossoms? Seid ihr denn Blumen?

1ST FLOWER 1ST GROUP

The garden's joy — Des Gartens Zier, —

1ST FLOWER 2ND GROUP

— its gentle fragrance, — — und duftende Geister, —

1ST FLOWERS 1ST AND 2ND GROUPS

— in spring plucked by our master! — — im Lenz pflückt uns der Meister! —

2ND FLOWERS 1ST AND 2ND GROUPS

We flourish here, — Wir wachsen hier, —

1ST FLOWERS 1ST AND 2ND GROUPS

— in summer and sunlight, — — in Sommer und Sonne, —

1ST AND 2ND FLOWERS 1ST AND 2ND GROUPS

— for you we blossom in gladness. — für dich erblühend in Wonne.

3RD FLOWERS 1ST AND 2ND GROUPS AND CHORUS I

You must be kind and true! Nun sei uns freund und hold!

2ND FLOWERS 1ST AND 2ND GROUPS AND CHORUS I

And give to the blossoms their due! Nicht karge den Blumen den Sold!

ALL FLOWER MAIDENS

If you cannot love us and cherish, Kannst du uns nicht lieben und minnen,
we'll wither and sadly we'll perish. wir welken und sterben dahinnen.

1ST FLOWER 2ND GROUP

Oh, hold me close to your heart! An deinen Busen nimm mich!

ALL FLOWER MAIDENS

Come! Handsome stranger! Komm'! holder Knabe!

1ST FLOWER 1ST GROUP

Your brow, oh, let me cool it! Die Stirn lass' mich dir kühlen!

CHORUSES I AND II

Let me for you blossom! Lass' mich dir erblühen!

2ND FLOWER 1ST GROUP

Soft cheeks, oh, let me stroke them! Lass' mich die Wange dir fühlen!

2ND FLOWER 2ND GROUP

Soft mouth, let me kiss it! Den Mund, lass' mich dir küssen!

1ST FLOWER 1ST GROUP

No! I! The fairest am I! Nein! Ich! Die Schönste bin ich!

2ND FLOWER 1ST GROUP

No! I am the fairest! Nein! Ich bin die Schönste!

CHORUSES I AND II

I am fairer! Ich bin schöner!

1ST FLOWER 2ND GROUP

No! I am more fragrant! Nein! Ich dufte süsser!

ALL THE OTHERS

No! I! I! Yes, I! Nein! Ich! Ich! — Ja, ich!

108

PARSIFAL
(gently moving them back)

You wild throng of blossoms enchanting, [57]   Ihr wild holdes Blumengedränge,
if I am to play with you, some space you [44, 57] soll ich mit euch spielen, entlasst mich der
must grant me!   Enge!

1ST FLOWER 2ND GROUP

Why do you scold?   [64]   Was zankest du?

PARSIFAL

Because you quarrel.   Weil ihr euch streitet.

1ST FLOWER 1ST GROUP THEN 2ND FLOWER 2ND GROUP

But only over you.   Wir streiten nur um dich.

PARSIFAL

Have done, then!   Das meidet!

2ND FLOWER 1ST GROUP

Let go of him: it's me he likes!   Du lass' von ihm: sieh', er will mich!

3RD FLOWER 1ST GROUP

Me rather!   Mich lieber!

3RD FLOWER 2ND GROUP

No, me!   Nein, mich!

2ND FLOWER 2ND GROUP

No, no, it's me he likes!   Nein, lieber will er mich!

1ST FLOWER 2ND GROUP

You're pushing me away?   Du wehrest mich von dir?

1ST FLOWER 1ST GROUP

You drive me away?   Du scheuchest mich fort?

2ND AND 3RD FLOWERS 1ST GROUP, 3RD FLOWER 2ND GROUP

Avoiding me?   Du wehrest mir?

CHORUS II

You're afraid of women?   Bist du feige vor Frauen?

ALL FLOWERS 2ND GROUP

Can't you trust yourself then?   Magst dich nicht getrauen?

CHORUS II

Can't you trust yourself then?   Magst dich nicht getrauen?

1ST FLOWER 1ST GROUP

How sad you're so cold and prudish!   [44]   Wie schlimm bist du Zager und Kalter!

BOTH CHORUSES

How sad! So shy?   Wie schlimm! So zag?

1ST FLOWER 2ND GROUP

How sad you're so cold and prudish!   Wie schlimm bist du Zager und Kalter!

CHORUS II

So shy and cold!   So zag und kalt!

1ST FLOWER 1ST GROUP

Would you have the butterfly wooed by   Die Blumen lässt du umbuhlen den
the flowers?   Falter?

109

So shy and cold! [64] Wie ist er zag!

2ND AND 3RD FLOWERS 2ND GROUP

So shy and cold! Wie ist er kalt!

CHORUS I

The fool won't awaken! Auf! Weichet dem Toren!

1ST AND 2ND GROUPS

By us he is forsaken. Wir geben ihn verloren.

CHORUS II

And so by us he's taken! Doch sei er uns erkoren!

2ND GROUP

No, he belongs to me! Nein, mir gehört er an!

ALL FLOWER MAIDENS

No, he belongs to us! Nein, uns gehöret er!
To us! Not you! To us, to us! Ja uns! Nein uns! Ja uns, ja uns!

PARSIFAL
(*half angrily, frightening the maidens off*)

No more! I'll not be caught! [57] Lasst ab! Ihr fangt mich nicht!

He is about to escape, when, hearing Kundry's voice out of the flower-foliage, he stands still in surprise.

KUNDRY

Parsifal! — Stay here! [54x] Parsifal! — Weile!

PARSIFAL

Parsifal . . .? [54x] Parsifal . . .?
So named me, dreaming one day, my So nannte träumend mich einst die Mutter.
mother.

At the sound of Kundry's voice, the maidens, terror-stricken, withdraw at once from Parsifal.

KUNDRY
(*gradually coming into sight*)

Here linger! Parsifal! Hier weile! Parsifal!
To greet you, gladness and joy are here. [58] Dich grüsset Wonne und Heil zumal.
You amorous children, leave him alone; [65] Ihr kindischen Buhlen, weichet von ihm;
fast-withering flowers, früh welkende Blumen,
be off, he was not sent for your sport. [44] nicht euch ward er zum Spiele bestellt.
Go home, tend to the wounded; Geht heim, pfleget der Wunden,
lonely awaits you many a knight. [39] einsam erharrt euch mancher Held.

The maidens, turning timidly and reluctantly away from Parsifal, withdraw to the palace.

1ST FLOWER THEN 3RD FLOWER, 2ND GROUP

Must I leave you! [44] Dich zu lassen!

2ND FLOWER 2ND GROUP

Must I lose you! Dich zu meiden!

3RD FLOWER THEN 1ST FLOWER, 1ST GROUP

Oh, what sorrow! Oh, wie wehe!

2ND FLOWER 1ST GROUP

Oh, sorrow and pain! Oh, wehe der Pein!

BOTH CHORUSES

Oh, sorrow! Oh, wehe!

110

From all I'd gladly part forever, — [64] Von Allen möchten gern wir scheiden, —

1ST AND 2ND GROUPS

— to be alone with you. — mit dir allein zu sein.

BOTH CHORUSES

Farewell! Farewell!	Leb' wohl! Leb' wohl!
You fair one, you proud one,	du Holder, du Stolzer,
you — fool!	du — Tor!

Laughing, the maidens disappear into the palace.

PARSIFAL

This garden — is it all a dream? [54] Dies alles — hab' ich nun geträumt?
He looks round timidly to the side whence the voice came. There appears through an opening of the flower-hedges a young and very beautiful woman — Kundry, in altered form — lying on a flowery couch, wearing a light veil-like robe of Arabian style.
Did you call to me, the nameless? [43] Riefest du mich Namenlosen?

KUNDRY

I named you, foolish pure one,		Dich nannt' ich tör'ger Reiner,
"Fal parsi", —	[54]	"Fal parsi", —
so pure and foolish: "Parsifal".		dich reinen Toren: "Parsifal".
So cried, in far Arabian land where he died,		So rief, als in arab'schem Land er verschied,
your father Gamuret to you, his son,	[42]	dein Vater Gamuret dem Sohne zu,
who in your mother's womb were stirring,		den er, im Mutterschoss verschlossen,
yes, thus he named you as he perished;		mit diesem Namen sterbend grüsste;
to tell these tidings I was waiting here:	[58, 31]	ihn dir zu künden, harrt' ich deiner hier:
what drew you here if not the wish to know?		was zog dich her, wenn nicht der Kunde Wunsch?

PARSIFAL

Ne'er saw I, nor dreamed before, what now [1h, 63] Nie sah ich, nie träumte mir, was jetzt
I see, and what has filled my heart with fear. ich schau', und was mit Bangen mich erfüllt.

Are you a flower grown in this lovely Entblüh'test du auch diesem
garden? Blumenhaine?

KUNDRY

No, Parsifal, you foolish pure one!	[4]	Nein, Parsifal, du tör'ger Reiner!
Far, far from here my homeland.		Fern, fern ist meine Heimat.
For you to find me, I lingered here awhile;	[65]	Dass du mich fändest, verweilte ich nur hier;
from far hence came I, many things I've seen.		von weit her kam ich, wo ich viel ersah.
I saw the child upon his mother's breast,	[65]	Ich sah das Kind an seiner Mutter Brust,
his early laughter lingers in my ear:		sein erstes Lallen lacht mir noch im Ohr:
her heart was grieving,	[58]	das Leid im Herzen,
but laughter inspired Herzeleide,		wie lachte da auch Herzeleide,
when, through her sorrows,		als ihren Schmerzen
on you, her son, her eyes she feasted.		zujauchzte ihrer Augen Weide.
On tender mosses you were cradled,	[65]	Gebettet sanft auf weichen Moosen,
your sleep was lulled with soft caresses;		den hold geschläfert sie mit Kosen,
in anxious vigil,	[58]	dem, bang in Sorgen,
your slumber was by your mother guarded;	[65]	den Schlummer bewacht der Mutter Sehnen,
and every morning		den weckt' am Morgen
a mother's glowing tears would wake you.		der heisse Tau der Muttertränen.
Forever weeping, born of sorrow,		Nur weinen war sie, Schmerzgebahren
she mourned your father's love and death:		um deines Vaters Lieb' und Tod:

111

as holy duty she decided
to save you from a fate like his.
From clash of arms, from men in deadly
conflict,
she ever strove to shield you and protect
you.
So anxious was she, ah! and fearful: [58]
no news of fighting arrived to disturb
you.
Can you remember her anxious cry
when late and far you were roaming?
Can you remember how she laughed
in relief when you had returned;
and how she caught you in her
embrace?
Oh, did you not fear her kisses then?

You were heedless of all her care, [16]
of all her anguished grieving,
when one day you did not return
and left no trace behind you.
Long days and nights she waited, [34a]
until her cries grew silent,
when grief consumed all the pain; [16]
for quiet death she yearned:
then sorrow broke her heart, [58]
and Herzeleide died.

vor gleicher Not dich zu bewahren,
galt ihr als höchste Pflicht Gebot.
Den Waffen fern, der Männer Kampf und
Wüten,
wollte sie still dich bergen und behüten.
Nur Sorgen war sie, ach! und Bangen:
nie sollte Kunde zu dir hergelangen.

Hörst du nicht noch ihrer Klage Ruf,
wann spät und fern du geweilt?
Was ihr das Lust und Lachen schuf,
wann sie suchend dann dich ereilt;
wann dann ihr Arm dich wütend
umschlang,
ward dir es wohl gar beim Küssen bang?

Doch, ihr Wehe du nicht vernahm'st,
nicht ihrer Schmerzen Toben,
als endlich du nicht wieder kam'st,
und deine Spur verstoben.
Sie harrte Nächt' und Tage,
bis ihr verstummt die Klage,
der Gram ihr zehrte den Schmerz,
um stillen Tod sie warb:
ihr brach das Leid das Herz
und Herzeleide starb.

PARSIFAL
(in growing surprise and alarm sinks down at Kundry's feet, overcome with distress)

Sorrow! Sorrow! What did I? Where was I? [41z] Wehe! Wehe! Was tat ich? Wo war ich?
Mother! Sweetest, dearest mother! [42, 43] Mutter! Süsse, holde Mutter!
Your son, your son was then your [16] Dein Sohn, dein Sohn musste dich
murderer! morden!
O fool! Blind and blundering fool! [34a] O Tor! Blöder, taumelnder Tor!
I wandered away, I could forget you, [7] Wo irrtest du hin, ihrer vergessend,
mother, I could forget you? [16] deiner, deiner vergessend?
Truest, dearest mother! Traute, teuerste Mutter!

KUNDRY

Had you not felt such grief, War dir fremd noch der Schmerz
then consolation's [25a] des Trostes Süsse
sweet relief you'd not know; labte nie auch dein Herz;
let sorrow that you feel, das Wehe, das dich reu't,
let torment yield die Not nun büsse
to the joy that love can reveal. im Trost, den Liebe dir beut.

PARSIFAL
(sinking lower in his sadness)

My mother, my mother, could I forget her! [16] Die Mutter, die Mutter, konnt' ich
vergessen!
Ha! What else did I also forget? [3] Ha! Was alles vergass ich wohl noch?
Have I remembered anything? Wess' war ich je noch eingedenk?
What else but folly lives in me? Nur dumpfe Torheit lebt in mir.

*Kundry, still reclining, bends over Parsifal's head, gently touches his forehead, and winds
her arm confidingly round his neck.* [36, 42]

KUNDRY

Acknowledge Bekenntnis
your fault and then it's ended; wird Schuld in Reue enden,
by knowledge Erkenntnis
your folly soon is mended. in Sinn die Torheit wenden.
Of love now learn the rapture [4, 36] Die Liebe lerne kennen,
that Gamuret once learned, die Gamuret umschloss,
when Herzeleide's passion [58] als Herzeleid's Entbrennen

within him fiercely burned!
For love that gave you [4]
life and being,
must death and folly both remove,
love sends
you now
a mother's blessing, greets a son [16]
with love's first kiss! [42]

ihn sengend überfloss!
Die Leib und Leben
einst dir gegeben,
der Tod und Torheit weichen muss,
sie beut
dir heut'
als Muttersegens letzten Gruss
der Liebe ersten Kuss!

She has bent her head completely over his and now presses her lips to his mouth in a long kiss. [4, 9, 1e, 1h, 41] Suddenly Parsifal starts up with a gesture of intense fear; his demeanour expresses some fearful change; he presses his hands tightly against his heart, as though to subdue a rending pain.

PARSIFAL

Amfortas!
The Spear-wound! — The Spear-wound! — [36]
It burns here in my heart! [45]
Oh! Torment! Torment! [41x]
Fearfullest torment,
the cry of anguish pierces my heart.
Oh! — Oh!
Keen anguish!
Piteous sufferer! [36]
The wound that I saw bleeding [1f, 1e]
is bleeding now in me!
Here — here! [41x, 36]
No! No! Not the Spear-wound is it. [4, 45]
Freely the blood may stream from my side! [4, 23]
Here! Here, a flame in my heart!
The yearning, the wild fearful
yearning
that fills my senses and holds them fast!
Oh! — pain of loving! [41x, 36]
How all things tremble, quiver and
shake
in sinful, guilty yearning!

Amfortas!
Die Wunde! — Die Wunde! —
Sie brennt in meinem Herzen!
O! Klage! Klage!
Furchtbare Klage,
aus tiefstem Herzen schreit sie mir auf.
O! — O! —
Elender!
Jammervollster!
Die Wunde seh ich bluten,
nun blutet sie in mir!
Hier — hier!
Nein! Nein! Nicht die Wunde ist es.
Fliesse ihr Blut in Strömen dahin!
Hier! Hier, im Herzen der Brand!
Das Sehnen, das furchtbare Sehnen,
das alle Sinne mir fasst und zwingt!
O! — Qual der Liebe!
Wie alles schauert, bebt und zuckt
in sündigem Verlangen!

While Kundry stares at him in fear and wonder, Parsifal appears to fall wholly into a trance. [25] He continues calmly.

This gaze is fixed now on the holy [8, 25]
Cup —
the sacred blood now glows: [1]
redemption's rapture, sweet and mild, [3]
to every heart brings all its healing:
but here — in this heart will the pain not [41x, 36]
lessen.
The Saviour's cry is stealing through [1i, 41x, 50]
me,
lamenting, ah, lamenting
for the profaned sanctuary:
"Redeem me, rescue me [1b, 10]
from hands defiled and guilty!" [1b, e]
Thus rang his lamentation,
fearful, loud, loud to my spirit. [1f, i]
And I, a fool, a coward, [60]
to childish deeds of daring fled away! [59]

Es starrt der Blick dumpf auf das
Heilsgefäss —
Das heil'ge Blut erglüht:
Erlösungswonne, göttlich mild,
durchzittert weithin alle Seelen:
nur hier — im Herzen will die Qual nicht
weichen.
Des Heilands Klage da vernehm' ich,
die Klage, ach die Klage
um das entweih'te heiligtum:
"Erlöse, rette mich
aus schuldbefleckten Händen!"
So rief die Gottesklage
furchtbar laut mir in die Seele.
Und ich — der Tor, der Feige,
zu wilden Knabentaten floh ich hin!

He throws himself despairingly on his knees. [3x]

Redeemer! Saviour! Lord of grace! [3, 9]
Can I my sinful crime efface?

Erlöser! Heiland! Herr der Huld!
Wie büss ich Sünder meine Schuld?

Kundry, whose astonishment has changed to sorrowful wonder, seeks hesitatingly to approach Parsifal.

KUNDRY

O noble knight! Cast off your fear! [66]
Look up and find redemption here!

Gelobter Held! Entflieh dem Wahn!
Blick' auf! Sei hold der Huldin Nah'n!

PARSIFAL

(still kneeling, gazes fixedly at Kundry, who during the following, bends over him with the caressing movements that she describes)

Yes! With these accents she called to him;	[35]	Ja! Diese Stimme! So rief sie ihm;
and with this look, — I seem to know it well,		und diesen Blick, deutlich erkenn' ich ihn,
and this one, with its remorseless laughter;		auch diesen, der ihm so friedlos lachte;
these lips too, yes, they tempted him thus,		die Lippe, ja so zuckte sie ihm,
she bent her neck toward him,		so neigte sich der Nacken,
thus boldly rose her head,		so hob sich kühn das Haupt;
thus fluttered her tresses around him,		so flatterten lachend die Locken,
thus twined she her arms round his neck —		so schlang um den Hals sich der Arm —
so tenderly his cheek caressing;	[4, 9]	so schmeichelte weich die Wange;
with all the powers of pain united,	[35]	mit aller Schmerzen Qual im Bunde,
his soul's salvation		das Heil der Seele
these lips once kissed away!	[41x, 36]	entküsste ihm der Mund!
Ha! — and her kiss!	[42]	Ha! dieser Kuss! —

Parsifal has gradually risen and pushes Kundry from him.

Destroyer! — Go from my side!	[4]	Verderberin! Weiche von mir!
Ever, ever be gone!	[36]	Ewig, ewig von mir!

KUNDRY
(very passionately)

Cruel man!	[66]	Grausamer!
If in your heart you feel		Fühlst du im Herzen
only others' sorrows,		nur andrer Schmerzen,
now feel what sorrows are mine!	[31]	so fühle jetzt auch die meinen!
If you're a saviour,	[66, 32]	Bist du der Erlöser,
then what restrains you		was bannt dich, Böser,
from joining with me in my salvation?	[34 a, b, c]	nicht mir auch zum Heil dich zu einen?
Through endless ages you I awaited,	[41x]	Seit Ewigkeiten harre ich deiner,
My saviour, ah! so late!		des Heilands — ach! so spät!
Whom once I dared revile!	[36]	den einst ich kühn geschmäht.
Oh! —		O! —
If you knew the curse	[58b]	Kenntest du den Fluch,
that holds through sleep and waking,		der mich durch Schlaf und Wachen,
through death and living,	[23]	durch Tod und Leben,
pain and laughter...		Pein und Lachen
To new afflictions newly steeled...	[41x, 36]	zu neuem Leiden neu gestählt,
endless torment racks my soul!	[16x, 10]	endlos durch das Dasein quält!
I saw Him — Him —	[1a, 8, 1f]	Ich sah Ihn — Ihn —
and mocked Him...	[34]	und lachte...
on me fell His look!	[41x, 50]	da traf mich sein Blick!
I seek Him now from world to	[1a, 8, 23x, 50, 41]	Nun such' ich ihn von Welt zu Welt,
world,		
till once more I behold Him.		ihm wieder zu begegnen.
In deepest woe —		In höchster Not —
I feel that He must be near,		wähn' ich sein Auge schon nah',
I see that look He gave.	[25]	den Blick schon auf mir ruh'n.
Then once more my accursed laughter fills me:	[34]	Da kehrt mir das verfluchte Lachen wieder:
a sinner sinks in my embraces!	[45]	ein Sünder sinkt mir in die Arme!
I laugh then, laugh then,	[34b]	Da lach' ich, lache,
I cannot weep,	[34d]	kann nicht weinen,
but crying, raving,	[7, 34b]	nur schreien, wüten,
storming, raging,		toben, rasen
I sink again into shameful night,		in stets erneuter Wahnsinns Nacht,
from which, remorseful, scarce I wake.	[23x, 36]	aus der ich büssend kaum erwacht.
One I desire with deathly yearning,	[1h]	Den ich ersehnt in Todesschmachten

one whom I knew, though I despised Him:
let me upon His breast lie weeping, [31]
for one brief hour with you united,
and then though God and world might scorn,
I'd be redeemed by you and reborn! [66]

den ich erkannt, den blöd' Verlachten:
lass mich an seinem Busen weinen,
nur eine Stunde mich dir vereinen,
und ob mich Gott und Welt verstösst,
in dir entsündigt sein und erlös't!

PARSIFAL

For evermore [36]
you'd be condemned with me,
for that brief hour,
forgetful of my calling, [54]
within your arms enfolded!
For your salvation I was sent,
if of your yearnings you repent.
The solace that can end your suffering
from purer fountains sweetly flows,
and grace will never be accorded
until the sinful fount you close. [43]
Another grace, another, yes! [41x]
For which in sorrow once I saw
the brothers pine: what cares distressed [8, 23x]
them,
what fear tormented and oppressed them!
But who with soul unclouded knows
that fount whence truly healing flows? [11]
Oh, anguish, — putting hope to flight! [41x]
O night of worldly error:
in quest of true salvation's light,
we drink damnation's draught of terror! [36, 4]

Auf Ewigkeit
wärst du verdammt mit mir,
für eine Stunde
Vergessens meiner Sendung
in deines Arms Umfangen!
Auch dir bin ich zum Heil gesandt,
bleibst du dem Sehnen abgewandt.
Die Labung, die dein Leiden endet,
beut nicht der Quell aus dem es fliesst,
das Heil wird nimmer dir gespendet,
eh' jener Quell sich dir nicht schliesst.
Ein And'res ist's, ein And'res, ach!
nach dem ich jammernd schmachten sah,
die Brüder dort, in grausen Nöten,
den Leib sich quälen und ertöten.
Doch wer erkennt ihn klar und hell,
des einz'gen Heiles wahren Quell?
O Elend, — aller Rettung Flucht!
O, Weltenwahns Umnachten:
in höchsten Heiles heisser Sucht —
nach der Verdammnis Quell zu schmachten!

KUNDRY
(*in wild ecstasy*)

So it was my kiss [63]
that made you see all these things clearly? [44]
The full embrace of my loving
surely to godhead will raise you.
Redeem the world then, if that's your task: [54]
become a god this moment,
let me be condemned for evermore,
my wound remain unclosed!

So war es mein Kuss,
der welthellsichtig dich machte?
Mein volles Liebes Umfangen
lässt dich dann Gottheit erlangen.
Die Welt erlöse, ist dies dein Amt:
schuf dich zum Gott der Stunde,
für sie lass mich ewig dann verdammt,
nie heile mir die Wunde!

PARSIFAL

Redemption, sinful one, I offer you. [57, 25]

Erlösung, Frevlerin, biet' ich auch dir.

KUNDRY
(*entreatingly*)

Then as a god let me love you, [44]
redemption you would bring to me.

Lass mich dich Göttlichen lieben,
Erlösung gab'st du dann auch mir.

PARSIFAL

Love and redemption will be granted, — [57, 25]
if the way
to Amfortas you now show.

Lieb' und Erlösung soll dir werden, —
zeigest du
zu Amfortas mir den Weg.

KUNDRY
(*breaking out in fury*)

No, — you'll never find him! [36]
He has fallen, so let him perish, [34c]
the unhallowed, [34d]
shame — welcomer,
whom I derided, — laughing —
laughing, —
Ha ha! Who fell by his own good Spear! [1h]

Nie — sollst du ihn finden!
Den Verfall'nen lass ihn verderben,
den Unsel'gen,
Schmachlüsternen,
den ich verlachte, — lachte — lachte —
Ha ha! Ihn traf ja der eig'ne Speer!

PARSIFAL

Who dared then to wound him with the [36]   Wer durft' ihn verwunden mit der heil'gen
sacred Spear?   Wehr?

KUNDRY

He — he —   Er — Er —
who once my laughter rebuked: der einst mein Lachen bestraft:
his curse, — ha! it gives me strength; [5]   Sein Fluch, ha, mir gibt er Kraft;
'gainst you yourself I'll summon the   gegen dich selbst ruf' ich die Wehr,
Spear
if for that sinner you dare to plead! — [44]   gibst du dem Sünder des Mitleids Ehr'! —
Ha, madness!   Ha, Wahnsinn!
                     (*beseechingly*)
Mercy! Mercy on me!   Mitleid! Mitleid mit mir!
And for one hour be mine! [32]   Nur eine Stunde mein!
For one brief hour be mine...   Nur eine Stunde dein...
To Amfortas   und des Weges
then I shall lead the way!   sollst du geleitet sein!

She tries to embrace him. He thrusts her forcibly from him.

PARSIFAL

Begone, accursed woman! [36]   Vergeh', unseliges Weib!

KUNDRY

She recoils in wild raging fury, and calls into the background.

Help me! Help me! To me! [44]   Hilfe! Hilfe! Herbei!
Seize the intruder! Oh help!   Haltet den Frechen! Herbei!
Bar him from leaving!   Wehrt ihm die Wege!
Guard every pathway! [34d]   Wehrt ihm die Pfade!
                (*to Parsifal*)
And though you should escape, and search [5]   Und flöhest du von hier, und fändest
through
every road in the world,   alle Wege der Welt,
the path that you seek,   den Weg, den du suchst
that path you'll never discover: des' Pfade sollst du nicht finden:
each road and pathway [4]   denn Pfad' und Wege,
that leads from my presence,   die dich mir entführen,
I now curse them to you: so verwünsch' ich sie dir:
Wander! Wander! [7x]   Irre! Irre!
Share in my fate! [41x]   Mir so vertraut!
Wander like me evermore!   Dich weih' ich ihm zum Geleit!
            [4]

Klingsor appears on the rampart and prepares to throw the Spear towards Parsifal. [36]

KLINGSOR

Halt there! I hold the weapon that will [7x]   Halt da! Dich bann' ich mit der rechten
serve!   Wehr!
The holy fool will fall by his master's [1h, 60]   Den Toren stelle mir seines Meisters
spear!   Speer!

He hurls the Spear, which remains hanging over Parsifal's head. [56, 25]

PARSIFAL
(*seizing the Spear, which he holds over his head*)

So with this Spear I vanquish your [25]   Mit diesem Zeichen bann' ich deinen
enchantment: Zauber:
and the wound shall be healed now   Wie die Wunde er schliesse,
by the Spear that wounded.   die mit ihm du schlugest,
To darkness and ruin   in Trauer und Trümmer
falls your deceiving display!   stürz' er die trügende Pracht!

He swings the Spear in the sign of the Cross; the Castle falls as by an earthquake. [36] *The garden withers to a desert;* [7] *the ground is scattered with faded flowers.* [44] *Kundry sinks down with a cry. Parsifal, hastening away, pauses on the top of the ruined wall, and turns back to Kundry.*

You know	Du weisst,
where once again you can find me when	wo du mich wieder finden kannst!
you choose!	

He hastens off. Kundry has raised herself a little and looks after him. [41x, 43]

Manfred Jung as Parsifal and Dunja Vejzovic as Kundry at Bayreuth in the production by Wolfgang Wagner, 1978 (photo: Festspielleitung Bayreuth)

Prelude. [47, 4, 6, 25, 36, 1h, 55, 38]

Act Three

The curtains open. Pleasant open spring landscape in the domain of the Grail. Flowering meadows rise gently towards the background. The edge of the forest is seen in the foreground, stretching away, right, to rising rocky ground. By the woodside a spring; and opposite this, further back, a hermit's hut, built against a mass of rock. Very early morning. Gurnemanz, grown very old and grey, and dressed as a hermit in the tunic of the Grail Knights, steps out of the hut and listens. [44, 47, 4]

GURNEMANZ

From there I heard the groaning.	[7]	Von dorther kam das Stöhnen.
So woefully moans no beast,		So jammervoll klagt kein Wild,
least of all today — this blessed and holy	[20]	und gewiss gar nicht am heiligsten
morn.		Morgen heut'.

A dull groaning is heard. [4, 23x]

I think I recognise that call of grief.		Mich dünkt, ich kenne diesen Klageruf.

He walks purposefully towards a thorn thicket at the side, much overgrown; he forces the undergrowth apart, then suddenly stops.

Ha! She back again?	[4]	Ha! Sie wieder da?
By wintry brambles and thorns		Das winterlich rauhe Gedörn'
she was concealed: how long now?	[5]	hielt sie verdeckt: wie lang' schon?
Up! Kundry! Up!		Auf! Kundry! Auf!
Now winter's fled, and spring is here!		Der Winter floh, und Lenz ist da!
Awaken! Awaken to spring! —		Erwache! Erwache dem Lenz! —

He draws Kundry stiff and lifeless out of the bushes, and bears her to a grassy mound nearby.

Cold and stiff!	[60]	Kalt und starr!
This time I truly fear she's dead:		Diesmal hielt ich sie wohl für tod:
and yet her groaning came to my ear?	[18b]	doch war's ihr Stöhnen, was ich vernahm?

As Kundry lies before Gurnemanz, he rubs her hands and temples, and does his utmost to relax her stiffness. [38] *At last life seems to awaken in her.* [44] *She is now fully awake, opens her eyes and utters a cry.* [25, 36] *She wears the coarse robe of a penitent, as in the first Act; her face is paler; the wildness has vanished from her looks and behaviour. She gazes long at Gurnemanz. Then, raising herself, she arranges her hair and dress, and moves away as though a serving maid.* [52, 18b]

How strange you are!		Du tolles Weib!
Have you no word for me?		Hast du kein Wort für mich?
Is this my thanks,	[26a]	Ist dies der Dank,
when from deathly slumber		dass dem Todesschlafe
I waken you once again?		noch einmal ich dich entweckt?

Kundry slowly bows her head; at length she speaks, hoarsely and brokenly. [52, 18b]

KUNDRY

Serving... serving.		Dienen... dienen.

GURNEMANZ
(shaking his head)

Your task will be but light:	[47]	Das wird dich wenig müh'n:
for now no messengers we need;	[5]	Auf Botschaft sendet sich's nicht mehr;
herbs and roots		Kräuter und Wurzeln
each of us finds for himself.		findet ein jeder sich selbst,
From beasts of the forest we learned.		wir lernten's im Walde vom Tier.

Kundry has meanwhile looked about her, sees the hut, and goes into it. Gurnemanz gazes after her, wondering.

How different from what she was before!	[26a]	Wie anders schreitet sie als sonst!
Can this holy day be the cause?	[25]	Wirkte dies der heilige Tag?
O day of mercy past comparing!	[8, 1f]	O! Tag der Gnade ohne gleichen!
In truth, for her salvation	[3]	Gewiss, zu ihrem Heile
I was allowed to wake		durft' ich der Armen heut'
this soul from deathly slumber.		den Todesschlaf verscheuchen.

Kundry returns from the hut; she carries a pitcher and goes with it to the spring. Here, glancing into the wood, she sees someone approaching in the distance, and turns to Gurnemanz to point this out to him. [28, 31] *He looks into the wood.*

Who comes toward the sacred spring? [57, 48, 42] Wer nahet dort dem heil'gen Quell?
In gloomy war apparel?   In düst'rem Waffenschmucke?
He is not one of our band!   Das ist der Brüder keiner!

During Parsifal's entry, Kundry fills her pitcher and moves slowly away into the hut, where she busies herself. Parsifal enters from the wood in a suit of black armour: with closed helm and lowered Spear he strides slowly forward, and moves with bowed head in dreamy uncertainty to the little grass mound beside the spring, where he seats himself. [47 & 5, 48]
Gurnemanz, having gazed long at Parsifal in astonishment, now steps towards him.

Hail there, my guest!   Heil dir, mein Gast!
Are you astray, and may I direct you?   Bist du verirrt, und soll ich dich weisen?
      Parsifal gently shakes his head. [47, 48]
No word of greeting to your host?   Entbietest du mir keinen Gruss?
      Parsifal bends his head. Gurnemanz continues, disconcerted.

Hey! — What! —   Heil! — Was? —
   Some vow perhaps   Wenn dein Gelübde
has constrained your lips to silence,   dich bindet mir zu schweigen,
but mine are bound to speak,   so mahnt das meine mich,
to tell you plainly, what is right.   dass ich dir sage, was sich ziemt.
This place you see is holy ground: [25]   Hier bist du an geweih'tem Ort:
a man should bear no weapons here,   da zieht man nicht mit Waffen her,
no vizored helmet, shield or spear;   [60]   geschloss'nen Helmes, Schild und Speer:
and least today! Do you not know   [25, 8]   und heute gar! Weisst du denn nicht,
   what holy day this is?   welch' heil'ger Tag heut' ist?
      Parsifal shakes his head.
No? From whence have you come?   Ja! Woher kommst du denn?
Among what heathens have you dwelt,   Bei welchen Heiden weiltest du,
   that you know not there dawns   zu wissen nicht, dass heute
on us now the all-holy Good Friday morn? [25, 8] der allerheiligste Karfreitag ist?
      Parsifal sinks his head yet lower.
Lay down your weapons!   [1e, i]   Schnell ab die Waffen!
Injure not the Lord, who this day,   Kränke nicht den Herrn, der heute,
bare of defence, His holy blood   bar jeder Wehr, sein heilig Blut
once shed to redeem the sinful world!   der sündigen Welt zur Sühne bot!

Parsifal raises himself after a further silence, thrusts his Spear into the ground before him, lays shield and sword beneath it, raises his vizor, and removing it from his head lays it with the other arms, and then kneels in silent prayer before the Spear. Gurnemanz watches Parsifal in wonder and emotion. He beckons to Kundry, who has just reappeared from the hut. [61, 18b, 57, 48]
Parsifal raises his eyes devoutly to the Spear-head. [3] *Gurnemanz addresses Kundry softly.*

You know him now?   Erkenn'st du ihn?
He it is who once the swan destroyed!   Der ist's der einst den Schwan erlegt!
      Kundry nods her head slightly. [1, 3]
In truth, 'tis he,   Gewiss, 's ist er,
the fool, whom I roughly turned away.   der Tor, den ich zürnend von uns wies.
      Kundry gazes fixedly but calmly at Parsifal. [1b, e]
Ha! By what pathway came he?   [1h, 55]   Ha! Welche Pfade fand er?
The Spear — I know it now.   Der Speer, — ich kenne ihn.
      (with great solemnity)
O holiest day   [3]   O! Heiligster Tag,
to which my soul is wakening!   [41]   an dem ich heut' erwachen sollt'!

Kundry has turned her face away. Parsifal rises slowly from prayer, looks calmly about him, recognises Gurnemanz, and extends his hand to him in greeting. [25, 8, 25]

PARSIFAL

Praise God! Once again I have found   Heil mir, das ich dich wiederfinde!
you!

GURNEMANZ

You still remember me?   [47]   So kennst auch du mich noch?
You still recall me,   Erkenn'st mich wieder,
whom grief and care have deeply bowed?   den Gram und Not so tief gebeugt?
How came you here — and whence?   [49]   Wie kam'st du heut — woher?

PARSIFAL

Through error and through suffering's [6]
   pathways came I;
and can I rightly think I can escape them,
    now that the forest's murmurs [40]
    once again I'm hearing,
and, good old man, again I greet you? ...
    Or — do I err still? [6]
    For everything seems altered.
	Der Irrnis und der Leiden Pfade kam ich,
	   soll ich mich denen jetzt entwunden
	   wähnen,
	    da dieses Waldes Rauschen
	    wieder ich vernehme,
	dich guten Greisen neu begrüsse? ...
	    Oder — irr' ich wieder?
	    Verändert dünkt mich alles.

GURNEMANZ

But say, who is it you are seeking?	So sag', zu wem den Weg du suchtest?

PARSIFAL

The man whose deepest anguish [45, 46x]
    in foolish wonder once I heard — [55]
    whom I can heal; I bring [1h]
his ordained salvation, as foretold. [47]
    But — ah! — [6]
the way of healing never finding,
   I wandered in error,
by a fearful curse led astray:
    numberless dangers, [38]
    battles and duels
forced me to leave the pathway, [6]
   even when I thought it was found.
Then I was seized with dread of failure, [60, 25]
   to keep the Spear unprofaned; [1h, 55]
so to defend it, and to guard it, [38]
I suffered many a wound on the way; [1h, 55]
    the Spear itself
    could not be wielded in battle;
    unprofaned
    at my side then I bore it;
    and home I now restore it: [25]
you see it shining pure and clear —
    the Grail's most holy Spear.
	Zu ihm, des tiefe Klagen
	    ich törig staunend einst vernahm, —
	    dem nun ich Heil zu bringen
	mich auserlesen wähnen darf.
	    Doch — ach! —
	den Weg des Heiles nie zu finden,
	   in pfadlosen Irren,
	trieb ein wilder Fluch mich umher:
	    zahllose Nöte,
	    Kämpfe und Streite
	zwangen mich ab vom Pfade,
	   wähnt' ich ihn recht schon erkannt.
	Da musste mich Verzweiflung fassen,
	   das Heiltum heil mir zu bergen,
	um das zu hüten, das zu wahren,
	ich Wunden jeder Wehr mir gewann;
	    denn nicht ihn selber
	    durft' ich führen im Streite,
	    unentweih't
	    führ' ich ihn mir zur Seite,
	    den nun ich heim geleite,
	der dort dir schimmert heil und hehr: —
	    des Grales heil'gen Speer.

GURNEMANZ
(in a transport of joy) [2]

O glory! Boundless grace! [8, 1f, 3] O wonder! Holy, highest wonder! [14]	O Gnade! Höchstes Heil! O! Wunder! Heilig hehrstes Wunder!

(to Parsifal, after somewhat composing himself)

O Lord! If it was a curse that drove you from the chosen path, be sure the spell is broken. You're standing in the Grail's domain, [25] our noble knights await you here. Ah, we have need of healing, [47] the healing that you bring! Since that morning when you first were here, the sorrow that you witnessed then, the anguish grew to direst need. Amfortas, maddened with the torment [45, 41x] he in soul and body suffered, [36] at last with raging defiance longed for [46x] death. No pleas, no sorrow of the brethren [49] could move him to fulfil his sacred office. The shrine lay shrouded, unrevealed the Grail:	O Herr! War es ein Fluch, der dich vom rechten Pfad vertrieb, so glaub', er ist gewichen. Hier bist du, dies des Grals Gebiet, dein' harret seine Ritterschaft. Ach, sie bedarf des Heiles, des Heiles, das du bringst! Seit dem Tage, den du hier geweilt, die Trauer, so da kund dir ward, das Bangen wuchs zur höchsten Not. Amfortas, gegen seiner Wunden, seiner Seele Qual sich wehrend, begehrt' im wütenden Trotze nun den Tod. Kein Fleh'n, kein Elend seiner Ritter bewog ihn mehr des heil'gen Amts zu walten. Im Schrein verschlossen bleibt seit lang' der Gral:

its guardian, racked with sinful suffering,
  who could not die so long
  as he beheld its light,
  thus hoped that he would perish,
and with his life thus end his cruel torment.
The food of Heaven we are now denied, [68, 49]
  and common fare must now support us:
and so there faded all our heroes' might. [33, 29, 42]
  No suppliants seek us now;
  no call to holy strife in distant countries:

  pale, dejected, wandering
and lost, and leaderless our knightly band. [47]
Here in the forest I have come to dwell,
  till death shall come to claim me,
as death my aged warrior-lord has claimed: [13]
  yes, Titurel, my holy King, [25]
when once the Grail's refreshment was denied him
  he died — a man, like others! [47]

so hofft sein sündenreu'ger Hüter,
  da er nicht sterben kann
  wann je er ihn erschaut,
  sein Ende zu erzwingen,
und mit dem Leben seine Qual zu enden.
Die heil'ge Speisung bleibt uns nun versagt,
  gemeine Atzung muss uns nähren:
darob versiegte uns'rer Helden Kraft.
  Nie kommt uns Botschaft mehr,
  noch Ruf zu heil'gen Kämpfen aus der Ferne:

  bleich und elend wankt umher
die mut- und führer-lose Ritterschaft.
In dieser Waldeck' barg ich selber mich,
  des Todes still gewärtig,
dem schon mein alter Waffenherr verfiel:
  denn Titurel, mein heil'ger Held,
den nun des Grales Anblick nicht mehr labte,
  er starb — ein Mensch, wie Alle!

PARSIFAL
(springing up in intense grief)

And I — I it is, [67]
who brought this woe on all!
  Ha! What transgression! [23x]
With a load of sin
must this my foolish head
eternally be laden,
for no repentance, no atonement [67, 42]
  my blinded eyes can lighten;
though chosen by God as a saviour, [55]
I lost myself in error;
salvation's only path has vanished!

Und ich, ich bin's,
der all dies Elend schuf!
  Ha! Welcher Sünden,
welches Frevels Schuld
muss dieses Toren Haupt
seit Ewigkeit belasten,
da keine Busse, keine Sühne
  der Blindheit mich entwindet,
zur Rettung selbst ich auserkoren,
in Irrnis wild verloren,
der Rettung letzter Pfad mir schwindet!

Parsifal seems about to fall senseless. Gurnemanz supports him, and lets him sink down onto the grassy mound. [67, 23x] Kundry hastily fetches a basin of water with which to sprinkle Parsifal. [32]

GURNEMANZ
(gently refusing Kundry)

Not that!
The holy spring itself [31,30]
must now refresh our pilgrim's brow. [27]
I feel some holy work [25]
he must today accomplish,
perhaps fulfil some sacred office:
let him be pure of stain, [19]
the dust of doubtful ways
our sacred spring can wash away!

Nicht so!
Die heil'ge Quelle selbst
erquicke uns'res Pilgers Bad.
Mir ahnt, ein hohes Werk
hab' er noch heut' zu wirken,
zu walten eines heil'gen Amtes:
so sei er fleckenrein,
und langer Irrfahrt Staub
soll nun von ihm gewaschen sein!

They both gently move Parsifal to the edge of the spring. [24] During the following Kundry unbinds the greaves of his armour, and Gurnemanz removes his breast-plate.

PARSIFAL
(gently and wearily)

This day to Amfortas shall I be guided? [68] Werd' heut' zu Amfortas ich noch geleitet?

GURNEMANZ
(still busy)

Most surely; for the lofty hall awaits:
the solemn funeral of my dearest lord [33, 69, 10]
  has summoned me today.

Gewisslich; uns'rer harrt die hehre Burg:
die Todenfeier meines lieben Herrn,
  sie ruft mich selbst dahin.

121

The Grail shall once more be to us revealed, [25]
    the long neglected office [49]
  shall once more be fulfilled,
to sanctify the noble father, [25]
who by his son's misdeed was slain;
the son would now atonement make:
this vow Amfortas swore.

Den Gral noch einmal uns da zu enthüllen,
    des lang versäumten Amtes
  noch einmal heut' zu walten,
zur Heiligung des hehren Vaters,
der seines Sohnes Schuld erlag,
die der nun also büssen will,
gelobt' Amfortas uns.

Parsifal gazes in quiet wonder at Kundry, who with eager humility is bathing his feet. [26a]

PARSIFAL
(to Kundry)

You washed my feet so humbly, [19]
now bathe for me my brow, good friend!

Du wuschest mir die Füsse,
nun netze mir das Haupt der Freund!

Gurnemanz takes some water in his hand from the spring and sprinkles Parsifal's head.

GURNEMANZ

Be purified, you pure one, by this water! [27]
It washes every guilt [24]
and care away from you!

Gesegnet sei, du Reiner durch das Reine!
So weiche jeder Schuld
Bekümmernis von dir!

During this Kundry draws a golden phial from her bosom, pours its contents over Parsifal's feet, and dries them with her hair, which she has hastily unbound. [27, 8, 32]

PARSIFAL
(gently taking the phial from her and passing it to Gurnemanz)

My feet you have anointed; [44]
my head now, friend of Titurel, anoint; [24]
this very day as King you shall acclaim me!

Du salbtest mir die Füsse,
das Haupt nun salbe Titurels Genoss,
dass heute noch als König er mich grüsse!

GURNEMANZ
(pouring the phial over Parsifal's head, upon which he lays his hands in blessing)

So truly it was promised; [57]
my blessing on your head,
as King I now acclaim you.
    O — pure one!
Pitying sufferer, [54]
all-wise deliverer!
You have redeemed him, torments you [23x]
    have suffered,
now lift the load forever from his head! [57, 25]

So ward es uns verhiessen;
so segne ich dein Haupt,
als König dich zu grüssen.
    Du — Reiner!
Mitleidsvoll Duldender,
heiltatvoll Wissender!
Wie des Erlös'ten Leiden du gelitten,
die letzte Last entnimm nun seinem
    Haupt!

PARSIFAL
Unnoticed, he has filled his hands with water from the spring, and now bends forward to Kundry, who is still kneeling before him, and pours it over her head.

My first of tasks I thus perform: — [27]
    baptized be, [25, 11]
  have faith in the Redeemer!

Mein erstes Amt verricht' ich so: —
    Die Taufe nimm,
  und glaub' an den Erlöser!

Kundry sinks her head to the earth; she seems to weep passionately. [41, 50] *Parsifal, turning away, gazes in gentle ecstasy upon field and forest, which are glowing in the morning light.* [60, 28]

Today the fields and meadows seem
  so fair!
Many a magic flower I've seen, [20]
which wildly sought to twine itself
  around me;
    but ne'er before so fair and mild
    the meadow flowers blooming;
  their scent recalls my childhood days
  and tells of loving trust to me.

Wie dünkt mich doch die Aue heut' so
  schön!
Wohl traf ich Wunderblumen an,
die bis zum Haupte süchtig mich
  umrankten;
    doch sah ich nie so mild und zart
    die Halme, Blüten und Blumen,
  noch duftet' all so kindisch hold
  und sprach so lieblich traut zu mir.

GURNEMANZ

It is Good Friday's magic, lord!

Das ist Karfreitags-Zauber, Herr!

O sorrow, that day of agony! [1a, 8]
When all creation, all that blooms,
that breathes, lives and lives anew, [1f]
should only sigh and sorrow.

O Wehe, des höchsten Schmerzentags!
Da sollte, wähn' ich, was da blüht,
was atmet, lebt und wiederlebt,
nur trauern, ach! und weinen.

GURNEMANZ

You see, it is not so. [28]
The sinner's tears of true repentance [8]
today with holy dew
bedeck the flowery mead [25]
and make them glow so brightly;
while all created things rejoice
to see the Saviour's sign of grace,
and raise a prayer to praise Him. [28]
Himself, the Saviour crucified, they see [1, 3]
not:
and so they raise their eyes to man
redeemed,
the man set free from sin, set free from [20]
terror,
by God's most loving sacrifice made pure:
today each blade and bloom upon the
meadow
knows well the foot of man will do no
harm;
in truth, as God with heavenly loving care [42, 43]
endured for man and for him bled,
so man now will repay that love
and walk with gentle tread. [28]
And grateful, all creation sings,
all things that bloom and pass away;
nature her innocence has won, [25]
all is renewed once more this day. [21]

Du siehst, das ist nicht so.
Des Sünders Reuetränen sind es,
die heut' mit heil'gem Tau
beträufet Flur und Au':
der liess sie so gedeihen.
Nun freut sich alle Kreatur
auf des Erlösers holder Spur,
will ihr Gebet ihm weihen.
Ihn selbst am Kreuze kann sie nicht
erschauen:
da blickt sie zum erlösten Menschen auf;
der fühlt sich frei von Sündenlast und
Grauen,
durch Gottes Liebesopfer rein und heil:
das merkt nun Halm und Blume auf den
Auen,
dass heut' des Menschen Fuss sie nicht
zertritt,
doch wohl, wie Gott mit himmlischer
Geduld
sich sein erbarmt' und für ihn litt,
der Mensch auch heut' in frommer Huld
sie schont mit sanftem Schritt.
Das dankt dann alle Kreatur,
was all' da blüht und bald erstirbt,
da die entsündigte Natur
heut' ihren Unschuldstag ewirbt.

Kundry has slowly raised her head, and gazes up with tearful eyes, filled with calm and earnest entreaty, at Parsifal. [20]

PARSIFAL

I saw them withering when once they [44]
mocked me:
are they now for redemption yearning? [8]
A dew of sorrow from your eyes is flowing: [41]
you're weeping . . . look, they smile, [28]
the meadows!

Ich sah sie welken, die einst mir lachten:
ob heut' sie nach Erlösung schmachten?
Auch deine Träne ward zum Segenstaue:
du weinest, sieh' — es lacht die Aue!

He kisses her gently on the forehead. [21, 8] A distant pealing of bells is heard. [30]

GURNEMANZ

Midday: [69]
the time has come.
Allow me, lord, as your squire to lead you!

Mittag:
die Stund' ist da.
Gestatte Herr, dass dein Knecht dich
geleite!

From the hut, Gurnemanz has fetched his Grail Knight's mantle, with which he and Kundry invest Parsifal. — Parsifal solemnly takes up the Spear and with Kundry follows Gurnemanz, who leads slowly. [29, 57] The scene changes very gradually, as in the first Act, but from right to left. After remaining for a time visible, the three entirely disappear, while the forest gradually vanishes, and in its place the rocks draw near. [69, 16, 47] Through the arched passages, the sound of bells swells ever louder. [30] The rock walls open, disclosing the lofty Grail Hall, as in the first Act, but without the feast-tables. Dusky light. From one side appear knights bearing Titurel's coffin, from the other side those escorting Amfortas in the litter, preceded by the covered shrine of the Grail. [69, 47]

(with Amfortas)

While we with sacred awe, concealed in [8] this shrine, the Grail escort to the altar, [25] concealed there in gloomy shrine, in mourning whom do you bear?	Geleiten wir im bergenden Schrein den Gral zum heiligen Amte, wen berget ihr im düst'ren Schrein und führt ihr trauernd daher?

2ND PROCESSION OF KNIGHTS
(with Titurel's body)

We bear a hero within this shrine, [29, 42] it holds the heavenly might, whom God Himself once chose as His guard: Titurel hither we bear. [8, 69]	Es birgt den Helden der Trauerschrein, er birgt die heilige Kraft, der Gott einst selbst zur Pflege sich gab: Titurel führen wir her.

1ST PROCESSION OF KNIGHTS

By whom was he killed, who, in God's own guard, God's self had in keeping?	Wer hat ihn gefällt, der, in Gottes Hut, Gott selbst einst beschirmte?

2ND PROCESSION OF KNIGHTS

He fell by the hand of conquering age, when the Grail's pure light was denied him.	Ihn fällte des Alters siegende Last da den Gral er nicht mehr erschaute.

1ST PROCESSION OF KNIGHTS

Who kept him the Grail's pure light from beholding?	Wer wehrt' ihm des Grales Huld zu erschauen?

2ND PROCESSION OF KNIGHTS

The man you're escorting, the Grail's sinful guardian.	Den dort ihr geleitet, der sündige Hüter.

1ST PROCESSION OF KNIGHTS

We escort him today because once more now, and once more only he'll fulfil his office. Ah, the final time! [47x]	Wir geleiten ihn heut', weil heut' noch einmal, zum letzten Male, will des Amtes er walten. Ach, zum letzten Mal!

Amfortas is now placed on the couch behind the Grail altar, the coffin is set down in front.
During the following, the knights turn to Amfortas.

2ND PROCESSION OF KNIGHTS

Sorrow! Sorrow! Guardian of the Grail, [30, 47x] the final time be your office performed!	Wehe! Wehe! Du Hüter des Grals, zum letzten Mal sei des Amtes gemahnt!

AMFORTAS
(wearily raising himself a little)

Yes — sorrow! Sorrow! Sorrow for me! [41x, 47] So cry I gladly with you: gladder still if you would deal me death, [49] for sin like mine small atonement.	Ja — Wehe! Wehe! Weh' über mich! So ruf' ich willig mit euch. Williger nähm' ich von euch den Tod, der Sünde mildeste Sühne.

The coffin is opened. [9] *All, at the sight of Titurel's corpse, break into a cry of woe.*
[45 & 36, 15] *Amfortas raises himself high on his couch, and turns to Titurel's corpse.*

My father! [15] Highly blessed among all heroes! You pure one, to whom once angels [14] descended: atttempting myself to die, I dealt you your death! Oh! You are now in glory on high [14] and behold the Saviour's face: —	Mein Vater! Hochgesegneter der Helden! Du Reinster, dem einst die Engel sich neigten: der einzig ich sterben wollt', dir gab ich den Tod! O! Der du jetzt in göttlichem Glanz den Erlöser selbst erschau'st —

124